DATE DUE

Modern Critical Views

GEOFFREY HILL

Modern Critical Views

GEOFFREY HILL

Edited with an introduction by

Harold Bloom

Sterling Professor of the Humanities
Yale University

1986
CHELSEA HOUSE PUBLISHERS
New York
New Haven   Philadelphia

PROJECT EDITORS: Emily Bestler, James Uebbing
ASSOCIATE EDITOR: Maria Behan
EDITORIAL COORDINATOR: Karyn Gullen Browne
EDITORIAL STAFF: Perry King, Bert Yaeger
DESIGN: Susan Lusk

Cover by Robin Peterson

Printed and bound in the United States of America

Library of Congress Cataloging in Publication Data

Geoffrey Hill.
    (Modern critical views)
    Bibliography: p.
    Includes index.
    1. Hill, Geoffrey—Criticism and interpretation—
Addresses, essays, lectures.   I. Bloom, Harold.
II. Series.
PR6015.I4735Z668   1986   821'.914   85-255114
ISBN 0–87754–669–X

Chelsea House Publishers
Harold Steinberg, Chairman and Publisher
Susan Lusk, Vice President
A Division of Chelsea House Educational Communications, Inc.
133 Christopher Street, New York, NY 10014

Contents

Editor's Note   ix

Introduction . . . . . .*Harold Bloom*   1

Beyond Modernism . . . . . .*Wallace D. Martin*.   11

The Poetry of Geoffrey Hill . . . . . .*Jon Silkin*   17

The Realism of Geoffrey Hill . . . . . .*Stephen Utz*.   41

An English Mason . . . . . .*Seamus Heaney*.   49

"The Tongue's Atrocities" . . . . . .*Christopher Ricks*   55

Creative Tact: *King Log* . . . . . .*William S. Milne*   69

The Idiom of *Mercian Hymns* . . . . . .*John Needham*   77

"Funeral Music" . . . . . .*Merle Brown*.   87

On Geoffrey Hill . . . . . .*Calvin Bedient*. 101

Hunter of Forms . . . . . .*A. K. Weatherhead*. 113

Being in Error . . . . . .*Eric Griffiths*. 129

The Mystery of the Charity of Charles Péguy
    John Hollander 137

Chronology 141

Contributors 143

Bibliography. 145

Acknowledgments. 147

Index 149

Editor's Note

This volume gathers together a representative selection of what, in the editor's judgment, is the best criticism so far devoted to the poetry of Geoffrey Hill. The editor's own essay, originally published as the introduction to *Somewhere Is Such a Kingdom* (1975), the American edition of *For the Unfallen, King Log* and *Mercian Hymns,* therefore surveys Hill's work only in those three books, and emphasizes his continuities with precursors in the Sublime mode.

After the "Introduction," this book's essays are reprinted in the chronological order of their original publication, beginning with Wallace D. Martin's early appreciation of *For the Unfallen* as a visionary genesis "beyond modernism." Another early assessment, by Hill's distinguished contemporary, the English poet, Jon Silkin, curiously but informedly centers upon the images of the work up through *Mercian Hymns.*

The brief essay on Hill's "realism" by Stephen Utz introduces the crucial question of just how so mannered a style can accommodate itself to Hill's quest, which is "to construct a realist totality" from "the fragments of our time and language."

Hill's most distinguished contemporary among the Irish poets, Seamus Heaney, accurately praises the *Mercian Hymns* as showing "Hill in full command of his voice." Christopher Ricks, examining Hill's diction with customary vigor and learning, relates Hill to some crucial analogues in T. S. Eliot's verse. In mode and procedure, Ricks is very nearly the archetype of what English criticism always threatens to become, an empiricist's descent into a kind of decaying "common sense," which is a characteristic also of Hill's own criticism.

The remarks by William S. Milne upon "creative tact" in *King Log,* and by John Needham on the idiom of *Mercian Hymns,* share a concern for Hill's obsessive uses of history, a concern that continues in Merle Brown's reading of "Funeral Music." Calvin Bedient provides a refreshing difference when he suggests that Hill manifests an Oedipal fear of his own poetic powers. In A. K. Weatherhead's "Hunter of Forms," we are stimulated again by yet another critical freshening, when the emphasis is placed upon metaphoric structures in Hill.

Eric Griffiths, reviewing Hill's criticism, judges it as the most important first book of that kind by a poet since T. S. Eliot's *The Sacred Wood*. This volume ends with John Hollander's brief but powerful meditation upon Hill's recent and majestic long poem, *The Mystery of the Charity of Charles Péguy*.

Introduction

Strong poetry is always difficult, and Geoffrey Hill is the strongest British poet now alive, though his reputation in the English-speaking world is somewhat less advanced than that of several of his contemporaries. He should be read and studied for many generations after they have blent together, just as he should survive all but a handful (or fewer) of American poets now active. Such canonic prophecy is founded on the authority of his best work, as I have experienced it in the fifteen years since the publication of *For The Unfallen*, his first book. From his first poem, appropriately "Genesis," on through the *Mercian Hymns*, Hill has been the most Blakean of modern poets. But this is deep or true influence, or Blake's Mental Warfare, rather than the easy transmission of image, idea, diction and metric that superficially is judged to be poetic influence. The merely extrinsic influences on Hill's early verse are mostly American; I can detect the fierce rhetoric of Allen Tate, and the visionary intensities of Richard Eberhart, in some places. Yet the true precursor is always Blake, and the War in Heaven that the strong poet must conduct is fought by Hill against Blake, and against Blake's tradition, and so against Hill himself.

As a war of poetry against poetry, Hill's work testifies to the repressive power of tradition, but also to an immensely individual and deeply moving moral protest against tradition. Like the hero he celebrates in his masterpiece, the *Mercian Hymns*, Hill is a martyrologist. His subject is human pain, the suffering of those who both do and sustain violence, and more exactly the daemonic relationship between cultural tradition and human pain. Confronted by Hill's best poems, a reader is at first tempted to run away, for the intellectual difficulty of the rugged, compressed verse is more than matched by the emotional painfulness and directness of Hill's vision. Hill does not comfort nor console, and offers no dialectic of gain through loss. His subject, like his style, is difficulty; the difficulty of apprehending and accepting moral guilt, and the difficulty of being a poet when the burden of history, including poetic history, makes any prophetic stance inauthentic. In more than twenty years of writing, Hill has given us three very slim volumes, not because his gift is sparse, but because he is too scrupulous to have allowed himself a less organized or less weighted utterance. There are no bad poems in Hill's three books, and so much is demanded of the reader, in concentration and in the dignity of a desperate humanism, that more productive poets are likely to seem too indulgent, by comparison. Hill does not indulge his reader, or himself, and just this remorseless concentration is Hill's assured greatness. The reader who persists will learn to read not only Hill, but other difficult and wholly indispensable poets as well, for only a poet as strong as Hill compels each of us to test his own strength as a reader and so to test and clarify also our own relation to tradition.

Tradition, Freud surmised, was the cultural equivalent of repressed material in the consciousness of the individual. The role of repression in poetry was misunderstood by Freud and has been misunderstood by most of his followers. Freud thought that sublimation was the psychic defense that *worked*, whether in life or in literature, while repression invariably failed, since repression augmented the unconscious. But poetry *is* figurative language, and in poetry sublimation is accomplished through the self-limiting trope of metaphor, while repression is represented by the expansive trope of hyperbole, with all of its Sublime glories and Grotesque dangers. From the viewpoint of poetry, the "unconscious mind" is an oxymoron, since repressed material in poetry has no place to go but up, onto the heights of what Romanticism called the Imagination. Romantic Imagination, whether in Blake or Coleridge, does not represent a return of the repressed, but is identical with the process of repression itself.

An individual poetic imagination can defend itself against the force of another imagination only by troping, so that a successful defense against poetic tradition always answers repression by an increase in repression. The return of the repressed is only an utopian or apocalyptic dream much indulged in by Marxist speculation, and by assorted contemporary shamans who inspire what is still being termed a counter-culture. Authentic poets show us that Emersonian Compensation is always at work in poetry as in life: nothing is got for nothing. What returns in authentic poetry is never the repressed, but rather the daemonic or uncanny element within repression, which poetic tradition has called by various names, including the Sublime, and the Imagination, both of them hyperbolical figurations for something that has no referential aspect or literal meaning, but that nevertheless guarantees the survival and continuity of poetic tradition. Poets and readers go on questing for one another in order to give a voice to this daemonic impulse that informs and purifies repression. "Purifies" here has no moral or spiritual meaning but refers rather to a process by which the daemonic is reconciled with the writing of poetry.

"Daemonic," in this sense, refers to a realm of power that invades the human world yet seems apart from human origins or human ends. In a very early poem, a visionary lyric in the mode of Eberhart, but like Eberhart reaching back to Blake's "Tyger," Hill laments the inadequacy of poetic language to tell his own experience of daemonic influx:

> I waited for the word that was not given,
>
> Pent up into a region of pure force,
> Made subject to the pressure of the stars;
> I saw the angels lifted like pale straws;
> I could not stand before those winnowing eyes
>
> And fell, until I found the world again.

Hill dislikes his early poems, yet they are not only permanent achievements but also quite essential for understanding all that comes after. "Genesis," for which he has a particular dislike, is superb in itself, a perfect "first" poem, and also a clear intimation of his largest debt to Blake's vision, which is the conviction that the Creation and the Fall were the same event. Another fine early poem, "In Memory of Jane Fraser" (which Hill evidently dislikes most, of all his work), speaks of a single, particular death as un-creating all of nature. For Hill, the natural world is, at best, "a stunned repose," a judgment that allies him to Blake rather than to Wordsworth, Shelley rather than to Keats. Hill's poem on the death of Shelley emphasizes the survival of the animal world, even as Shelley, the Modern Poet proper, or New Perseus, quests aimlessly, "clogged sword, clear, aimless mirror —/With nothing to strike at or blind/in the frothed shallows."

The themes and procedures of both Hill's books of short poems are summed up in what I judge to be his best single poem, the double-sonnet called "Annunciations." Though Hill transcends his own earlier mode in *Mercian Hymns* (as will be seen), "Annunciations" is so important a poem that I will discuss it at some length. A reader who can interpret "Annunciations" can learn to interpret the rest of Hill, and also acquire many insights that will aid in reading any truly difficult poetry of the Post-Romantic tradition. For, in "Annunciations," Hill wrote what later tradition may judge to have been the central shorter poem of his own generation, a poem that is itself a despairing poetics, and a total vision both of natural existence, and of the necessary limitations of what we have learned to call imagination.

An "annunciation" can be any proclamation, but despite Hill's plural title, the reverberation here depends upon the Annunciation proper, the announcement of the Incarnation by the Angel Gabriel in

Luke 1:26–38. In some grim sense, Hill's starting-point is the festival (25 March) celebrating Gabriel's announcement. But "the Word" here is not the Logos, nor simply the words of poetry, all poetry, but the idealization of poetry that is so pervasive in Western tradition:

> The Word has been abroad; is back, with a tanned look
> From its subsistence in the stiffening-mire.
> Cleansing has become killing, the reward
> More touchable, overt, clean to the touch.

This Word seems more a tourist than an Eliotic explorer; indeed a hygienic tourist-hunter. Returned, the questers sit together at a literary feast with their scholarly and critical admirers:

> Now, at a distance from the steam of beasts,
> The loathly neckings and fat shook spawn
> (Each specimen-jar fed with delicate spawn)
> The searchers with the curers sit at meat
> And are satisfied.

I do not know how to interpret this except as an attack upon everyone who has to do with poetry: poets, critics, teachers, students, readers. It is as though Yeats, after observing in vision his nymphs and satyrs copulating in the foam, his Innocents re-living their pain and having their wounds opened again, then attended a banquet in honor of his "News for the Delphic Oracle." The poem becomes a "specimen-jar," holding an aesthetic reduction of copulation and bleeding wounds. Is such an attack as Hill's legitimate, since it would apply as much to Homer as to any other poet? Is Hill attacking a false idealization of poetry or the *Ananke* that governs all poetry? The remainder of the first part of "Annunciations" will not answer these questions:

> Such precious things put down
> And the flesh eased through turbulence, the soul
> Purples itself; each eye squats full and mild
> While all who attend to fiddle or to harp
> For betterment, flavour their decent mouths
> With gobbets of the sweetest sacrifice.

Primarily this is Hill's uncompromising attack upon himself, for more even than Yeats, or even his contemporary Ted Hughes, he writes a poetry whose subject is violence and pain, thus accepting the danger of easing the flesh through a vision of turbulence. Much of the success with readers, particularly British readers, of the later Yeats and of Hughes is surely based upon feeding the reader's eye with imaginary lust and suffering until that eye "squats full and mild." Hill's attack upon "all who attend to fiddle or to harp/For betterment" is therefore an attack upon the most traditional, Aristotelian defense of poetry, an attack upon the supposed function of catharsis. Poems are "gobbets of the sweetest sacrifice," and readers flavor their mouths decently even as decent Christians swallow the bread of communion. It becomes clear that Hill is attacking, ultimately, neither poetry nor religion, but the inescapable element that always darkens tradition, which is that the living, feeding upon the repressions of the dead, repress further and so become the sustenance of the dead. Hill's "sacrifice" is what Nietzsche and Freud would have termed an Antithetical Primal Word, for it is debatable whether the victims commemorated by the poem, or the readers, are the "sacrifice."

The Antithetical Primal Word of the second part of "Annunciations" is of course "love," and here the majestic bitterness of the Sublime triumphs in and over Hill:

> O Love, subject of the mere diurnal grind,
> Forever being pledged to be redeemed,
> Expose yourself for charity; be assured
> The body is but husk and excrement.
> Enter these deaths according to the law,
> O visited women, possessed sons! Foreign lusts
> Infringe our restraints; the changeable
> Soldiery have their goings-out and comings-in
> Dying in abundance. Choicest beasts
> Suffuse the gutters with their colourful blood.
> Our God scatters corruption. Priests, martyrs,
> Parade to this imperious theme: 'O Love,
> You know what pains succeed; be vigilant; strive
> To recognize the damned among your friends.'

If I could cite only one stanza by Hill as being wholly representative of him, it would be this, for here is his power, his despair and (in spite of himself) his Word, not in the sense of Logos but in the Hebraic sense of *davhar*, a word that is also an act, a bringing-forward of something previously held back in the self. This Word that rejects being a Word is a knowing misprision or mis-taking of tradition, but even the most revisionary of Words remains a Word, as Hill doubtless knows. Being willing to go on writing poems, however sparsely, is to believe that one possesses a Word of one's own to bring forward. When Hill says, "Our God scatters corruption," he means that the God of lovers (and of poets) is antithetical to Himself, that this God is the ambivalent deity of all Gnostics. I take it that "scatters" does not mean "drives away" but rather "increases" corruption by dispersal, which implies that "corruption" takes something of its root-meaning of "broken-to-pieces." Hill's subject then is the Gnostic or Kabbalistic "Breaking of the Vessels," the Fall that is simultaneously a Creation, as in his first, Blakean, chant-poem "Genesis."

Part II of "Annunciations" is thus more of a proclamation against Love than a prayer to Love. Love, addressed under its aspect of repetition, is urged to more honesty, and to a reductive awareness of the body. Corporeal passion lives and dies according to the old dispensation, or law, but Hill comes to proclaim a new Incarnation, which is only a Gnostic dying into yet more sexual abundance. As an incessant martyrologist, Hill grimly announces the imperious as against the imperial or Shakespearean theme. Love, who knows that pains only succeed or follow one another (but are never successful), is urged at least to distinguish its true martyrs among the panoply of its worshippers, and so recognize accurately its valid theme.

Repeated readings of "Annunciations" should clarify and justify Hill's densely impacted style, with its reliance upon figurations of Hyperbole. Hill's mode is a negative or counter-Sublime, and his characteristic defense against the tradition he beautifully sustains and extends is an almost primal repression:

> Not as we are but as we must appear,
> Contractual ghosts of pity; not as we
> Desire life but as they would have us live,
> Set apart in timeless colloquy:
> So it is required; so we bear witness,
> Despite ourselves, to what is beyond us,
> Each distant sphere of harmony forever
> Poised, unanswerable . . .

This is again a Gnostic sublimity. Blake could still insist that pity survived only because we kept on rendering others piteous, but Hill comes later, and for him the intoxication of belatedness is to know that our reality and our desire are both negated by our appearance as legatees. It is tradition that makes us into "contractual ghosts of pity." A Beautiful Necessity represses us, and makes us bear witness to a dead but still powerful transcendence. Hill characterizes one of his sequences as "a florid grim music" or an "ornate and heartless music punctuated by mutterings, blasphemies and cries for help." A baroque pathos seems to be Hill's goal, with the ornateness his tribute to tradition, and the punctuation of pathos his outcry against tradition. Hill's is clearly a poetics of pain, in which all the calamities of history become so many poetic salutes, so many baroque meditations, always trapped in a single repetition of realization. Man is trapped "between the stones and the void," without majesty and without justice except for the errors of rhetoric, the illusions of poetic language. Like his own Sebastian Arrurruz, Hill's task is "to find value/In a bleak skill," the poet's craft of establishing true rather than false "sequences of pain."

"It must give pleasure," Stevens rightly insisted, and any critic responding to Hill should be prepared to say how and why Hill's poetry can give pleasure, and in what sense Hill's reader can defend himself from being only another decent mouth opened wide for the poetry-banquet. How is the reader to evade becoming "the (supposed) Patron" so bitterly invoked in the final poem of Hill's first book? The Gnostic answer, which is always a latecomer's answer, is that the reader must become not a patron but one of those unfallen who gave Hill's first book its title:

> For the unfallen—the firstborn, or wise
> Councillor—prepared vistas extend
> As far as harvest; and idyllic death
> Where fish at dawn ignite the powdery lake.

The final trope here is perhaps too Yeatsian, but the previous trope that gives back priority to the unfallen has a more High Romantic tenor, looking back to Keats' vision of Autumn. Hill cannot celebrate natural completion, but he always finds himself turning again "to flesh and blood and the blood's pain" despite his Gnostic desire to renounce for good "this fierce and unregenerate clay." Of his incessant ambivalence, Hill has made a strong poetry, one that battles tradition on tradition's own terms, and that attempts to make of its conscious belatedness an earliness. The accomplished reader responds to Hill's work as to any really strong poetry, for the reader too needs to put off his own belatedness, which is surely why we go on searching for strong poetry. We cannot live with tradition, and we cannot live without it, and so we turn to the strong poet to see how he acts out this ambivalence for us, and to see also if he can get beyond such ambivalence.

Hill begins to break through his own dialects of tradition in *Mercian Hymns*, the sequence of prose-poems he published on the threshold of turning forty. His hero is Offa, an eighth century Midlands "king," who merges both into a spirit of place and into the poet celebrating him, particularly the poet-as-schoolboy, for *Mercian Hymns* is a kind of *Prelude*-in-little. Yet here the growth of a poet's mind is not stimulated by nature's teachings, but only by history and by dreams. Transcendence, for Hill, returned or re-entered the sublunary world in old tapestries, sculpture, and metal-work, but mostly in historicizing reverie, which is the substance of these hymns. With *Mercian Hymns*, Hill rather triumphantly "makes it new," and though the obsession with tradition is as strong, much of the ambivalence towards tradition is miraculously diminished. Indeed, certain passages in *Mercian Hymns* would approach sentimentality if the poet did not remain characteristically condensed and gnomic, with the familiar spectre of pain hovering uncannily close:

> We have a kitchen-garden riddled with toy-shards,
> with splinters of habitation. The children shriek
> and scavenge, play havoc. They incinerate boxes,
> rags and old tyres. They haul a sodden log, hung
> with soft shields of fungus, and launch it upon
> the flames.

Difficult as Hill was earlier, *Mercian Hymns*, despite the limpidity of its individual sections, is the subtlest and most oblique of his works. It is not only hard to hold together, but there is one question as to what it is "about," though the necessary answer is akin to *The Prelude* again; Hill has at last no subject but his own complex subjectivity, and so the poem is "about" himself, which turns out to be his exchange of gifts with the Muse of History (section X). I suggest that the structure and meaning of *Mercian Hymns* is best approached through its rhetoric, which as before in Hill is largely that of metaleptic reversal or transumption, the dominant trope of Post-Romantic poetry in English. For a full analysis of the trope and its poetic history, I must refer to my book, *A Map of Misreading* and give only a brief account here. Transumption is the trope of a trope, or technically the metonymy of a metonymy. That is, it tends to be a figure that substitutes an aspect of a previous figure for that figure. Imagistically, transumption from Milton through the Romantics to the present tends to present itself in terms of earliness substituting for lateness, and more often than not to be the figure that concludes poems. Translated into psychoanalytic terms, transumption is either the psychic defense of introjection (identification) or of projection (refusal of identity), just as metaphor translates into the defense of sublimation, or hyperbole into that of repression. The advantage of transumption as a concluding trope for belated poems is that it achieves a kind of fresh priority or earliness, but always at the expense of the presentness of the present or living moment. Hill is as transumptive a poet, rhetorically, as Milton or Wordsworth or Wallace Stevens, and so he too is unable to celebrate a present joy.

There is no present time, indeed there is no self-presence in *Mercian Hymns*. Though Hill's own note on the sequence betrays some anxiety about what he calls anachronisms, the genius of his work excludes such anxiety. Nothing can be anachronistic when there is no present:

> King of the perennial holly-groves, the riven sand-
> stone; overlord of the M5: architect of the historic
> rampart and ditch, the citadel at Tamworth,
> the summer hermitage in Holy Cross: guardian of
> the Welsh Bridge and the Iron Bridge: contractor
> to the desirable new estates: saltmaster: money-
> changer: commissioner for oaths: martyrologist:
> the friend of Charlemagne.
>
> 'I liked that,' said Offa, 'sing it again,'

It is not that Offa has returned to merge with the poet, or that Hill has gone back to Offa. Hill and Offa stand together in a figuration that has introjected the past and the future, while projecting the present. Hill's epigraph, from the neglected poet and essayist, C. H. Sisson, analogizes his own conduct as private person and Offa's conduct of government, in all aspects of conduct having to do with "object and justification." Hill's struggle, as person and as poet, is with the repressive power of tradition, with the anxieties of history. Offa is seen by Hill as "the starting-cry of a race," as the master of a Primal Scene of Instruction, an imposition of order that fixates subsequent repression in others, which means to start an inescapable tradition. By reconciling himself with Offa, Hill comes close to accepting the necessary violence of tradition that earlier had induced enormous ambivalences in his poetry.

This acceptance, still somber but no longer grim, produces the dominant tone of Mercian Hymns, which is a kind of Wordsworthian "sober coloring" or "still sad music of humanity." But the sequence's vision remains Blakean rather than Wordsworthian, for the world it pictures is still one in which Creation and Fall cannot be distinguished, and at the end Offa is fallen Adam or every man: "he left behind coins, for his lodging, and traces of red mud." The reader sees that each hymn is like the inscription on one of Offa's hammered coins, and that these coins are literally and figuratively the price of a living tradition, its perpetual balance of Creation and Fall. Hill has succeeded, obliquely, in solving his aesthetic-moral problem as a poet, but the success is as equivocal and momentary as the pun on "succeed" in "Annunciations." Hill now knows better "what pains succeed," and his moving sequence helps his readers to the same knowledge.

No critical introduction to a poet only just past forty in age can hope to prophesy his future development. I have seen no poems written by Hill since Mercian Hymns, but would be surprised if he did not return to the tighter mode of For The Unfallen and King Log, though in a finer tone. His achievement to date, as gathered in his volume, seems to me to transcend the more copious work of his contemporary rivals: Hughes, Gunn, Kinsella, Tomlinson, Silkin. Good as they are, they lack poetic strength when compared with Hill. He has the persistence to go on wrestling with the mighty dead—Blake, Wordsworth, Shelley, Yeats—and to make of this ghostly struggle a fresh sublimity. He is indeed a poet of the Sublime, a mode wholly archaic yet always available to us again, provided a survivor of the old line come to us:

> Against the burly air I strode,
> Where the tight ocean heaves its load,
> Crying the miracles of God.

WALLACE D. MARTIN

Beyond Modernism

By blood we live, the hot, the cold,
To ravage and redeem the world:
There is no bloodless myth will hold.

And by Christ's blood are men made free
Though in close shrouds their bodies lie
Under the rough pelt of the sea;

Though Earth has rolled beneath her weight
The bones that cannot bear the light.

—from "Genesis"

In Geoffrey Hill's "Genesis," a visionary poet gives an acanonical account of the Creation as an event in which he participated (in its first published version the poem was subtitled "a ballad of Christopher Smart"). His first act is to bring the sea "to bear/ Upon the dead weight of the land." By naming, the poet creates: the sea is relevant to (bears upon) the land because he speaks. At the same time, the physical creation is taking place. The sea presses down on the land and brings forth life there (two other senses of "to bear"); life necessitates bloodshed, and at the end of the poem, quoted above, the dead return to the sea. Those who "cannot bear the light" are those who cannot endure apparent or transcendent truths and/or those who have been unable to produce or sustain transcendent illumination. A myth based on blood can endure, but if understood it may not be bearable.

From *Contemporary Literature* 4, vol. 12 (Autumn 1971). Copyright © 1971 by the Regents of the University of Wisconsin.

Christianity, myth, history, the sea, love, and death: most of Hill's early poems are constituted from permutations of these few themes. The sea-burial of "Genesis" recurs throughout *For the Unfallen*. The Plantagenet kings lie in their graves before judgment day, before "sleeked groin, gored head,/Budge through the clay and gravel, and the sea/Across daubed rock evacuates its dead." The dead Jews of Europe lie "subdued under rubble, water, in sand graves" and "the sea flickers, roars, in its wide hearth." "Those varied dead! The undiscerning sea/Shelves and dissolves their flesh as it burns spray," and a dead lover is "hammocked in salt tagged cloth/ That to be bleached or burned the sea casts out." (Further examples could be taken from five other poems in which death at sea is the central subject, but enough have been cited to indicate the pervasiveness of the image and to explore its significance.) In traditional analyses of thematic imagery, the meaning of an image emerges only after a number of instances have been collated, particulars leading to generalization. But the paradoxical implications of death at sea are evident in one of Hill's earliest poems, even to those not acquainted with Phlebas the Phoenician; the image is an archetype from the beginning. Perhaps, then, the archetype takes on different meanings in particular contexts, the movement of significance being from general to particular.

"Metamorphoses," one of the longer poems in *For the Unfallen*, exemplifies the relationship between death at sea and Hill's other thematic preoccupations. The protean "Metamorphoses" are a collage of five sections related to one another through overlapping themes and allusions to animals associated with Venus. In the second section, a poet who feels he has been made a scapegoat receives sympathetic counsel on how to get ahead in the literary world. The he-goat, like other tireless breeders, was sacred to Venus. In the third section, entitled "The Re-Birth of Venus," the goddess is reincarnated as a shark after the Flood and in an estuary "approaches all/ Stayers, and searchers of the fanged pool." The sea-dead are the subject of section four, the title of which, "Drake's Drum," is the only indication that the poem is to be understood as a warning that England is endangered. In the last section a lover is separated from his love, commits suicide, and ends in the sea, "seeking that love flesh dared not answer for." It is possible to read the sequence as a symbolist poem involving the progress of the poet from bewildered naiveté to the realization that true love and song are possible only in the fate of Orpheus; there is not however enough symbolic implication to sustain even this interpretation.

By comparison, the collage technique of *Hugh Selwyn Mauberley* is relatively transparent. Hill's Venus is not transformed into an aesthetic curio, like Pound's ("Medallion"); she remains goddess, archetypal and powerful, but in her association with the sea acquires its destructive as well as its generative potential. The Venus of Baudelaire's "Un Voyage à Cythère" is perhaps a precedent. Life originated in the sea, yet in the story of the Flood is destroyed by it; the love that arises with Venus springs from the castration of Uranus. The meaning of the poem is created through juxtaposition of archetypes that are referentially associated but traditionally segregated because when combined they tend to negate one another. The poet has intervened in an inherited tradition only insofar as he has selected its materials to reveal their incoherence, while welding them together in a traditional yet distinctive and powerful style. What is revealed is not that "the center cannot hold" but that there never was a center, except in Yeats's system, and never a still point, except in Eliot's imagination.

The example of *Hugh Selwyn Mauberley* is apposite to "Of Commerce and Society," a six-poem sequence in which the death of Shelley and the loss of the Titanic appear amid records of two world wars and the cultural history of the continent that produced them. Various aspects of death at sea are evoked in particular contexts, just as the sea itself can be terrible or benign, give life or take it away, act as instrument of divine justice or instance of pointless destruction. Likewise with the themes of love, history, myth: their energies are centrifugal, and, always meeting in strife, they never coalesce in an enduring pattern. Critics who have complained about the obscurity of Hill's poems have understood them but misunderstood their purpose. From Northrop Frye we learned that all poetry is archetypal. Hill reveals that the archetypes themselves are compounded of irreconcilable elements; that those who find in them experiential or aesthetic unity have misunderstood them; that history offers continual testimony to the incoherence of reality; that any art work glossing over these facts is a lie. History cannot be "scraped clean of its old price," though it can be rewritten or forgotten.

Nearly all of the unresolved tensions in Hill's poetry are represented in the following lines describing a saint depicted in stained glass: "In the sun lily-and-gold-coloured,/Filtering the cruder light, he has endured,/A feature for our regard; and will keep;/Of worldly purity the stained archetype." In art, at least, the saint endures; but the artistic medium itself does dubious justice to what he supposedly represents because it filters the light and stains it. The contradictions inherent in archetypes are paralleled by those inherent in language. In order to represent the latter, Hill has written a number of poems that can be exhaustively explicated—yielding two opposed meanings. The result cannot be characterized as "ironic" because no

single word or attitude can hold the meanings together. The verbal ambiguities of *For the Unfallen* are deliberate but they are seldom sustained
through an entire poem. Systematic ambiguity, whereby every assertion
denies itself, is achieved in his "Annunciations," which appear in *The
Penguin Book of Contemporary Verse* along with an explication that he
prepared for the puzzled anthologizer.

Hill dismembers his subject matter, his poetry, and poetry as a whole
in "History as Poetry":

> Poetry as salutation; taste
> Of Pentecost's ashen feast. Blue wounds.
> The tongue's atrocities. Poetry
> Unearths from among the speechless dead
>
> Lazarus mystified, common man
> Of death. The lily rears its gouged face
> From the provided loam. Fortunate
> Auguries; whirrings; tarred golden dung:
>
> "A resurgence" as they say. The old
> Laurels wagging with the new: Selah!
> Thus laudable the trodden bone thus
> Unanswerable the knack of tongues

Poetry may be salutation to the Muses or the patron; the salutation of our
Lady, the Annunciation; the Pentecostal tongues of fire burning where they
do not inspire. The atrocities of our tongue (language) are not only those
recorded in our history but those of poets, who are criminal when they
misrepresent history and unforgivable when they write atrocious verse.
Inspired tongues have also led to Christian atrocities. The lily of Mary, the
Resurrection, and poetry feeds on the loam provided by the dead. Thus
history nourishes a mendacious artistic beauty; but the relationship between
life and death is no more benign in nature or religion. "Selah," presumed
to be a stage direction for performers of the Psalms, is an ancient counterpart
of the shoptalk exchanged by old and young poets, but the resurgence of
poetry (heralded by the English press) is not a rising again of song to the
Most High or a resurrection. The Christian paradigm of poetry is not of
course without ambiguities: Lazarus is understandably mystified to be alive
and/or his story is unacceptably mystifying. And so on—almost endlessly.
If we accept the terms of the argument—that history, religion, and poetry
are inescapably interrelated—poetry can only embody unresolvable tensions
and cast doubt on its means of doing so. These tensions are implicit in the
poet's medium and materials; he either exposes them or attempts to conceal
them.

Hill, like Middleton, returns in his poetry with an unmannerly insistence to those atrocities of recent history that "might better be forgotten" since they cannot be understood. Unlike Eliot, he does not compare the present unfavorably with the past; neither is given an advantage. But an emphasis on the negative implications of Hill's poetry is misleading if its context and intention are forgotten. He did not create Western history or its traditions; although thought and feeling are (inevitably) manifest in his choice of thematic materials, he deliberately avoids reference to his own experience and in this sense is impersonal. While constantly returning to history, he recognizes the division between event and verbal representation as absolute. But within the linguistic sphere to which he is confined, the poet can—and should—accept his artistic heritage, insure its preservation, and enlarge it insofar as he is able. To preserve poetry, it is necessary to preserve language from complacency, mendacity, and indifference. By exposing the contradictions that lie just below the conventional surface of linguistic usage, the poet safeguards meaning and the possibility of creation. Both depend on differentiation, whereby relations can be established; the alternative is chaos, a unity without meaning.

By submitting himself completely to the imperatives of tradition, Hill has been able to reveal its incoherence. Having done so, he tentatively explores the possibility of subverting his accomplishment by attributing it to a partial consciousness. In "Funeral Music," a group of eight poems on the Wars of the Roses, existence is tested in relation to imagined alternatives ("Suppose all reconciled/By silent music"); the endeavor to represent the past impersonally is seen as subject to personal compulsions ("What I dare not is a waste history/Or void rule"); the seeming inevitability of historical patterns does not encompass being in the present ("Not as we are but as we must appear . . . not as we/Desire life but as they would have us live"). The love lyrics that Hill attributes to an apocryphal Spanish poet in "The Songbook of Sebastian Arrurruz" testify to the significance of what history does not preserve. This lovelorn Sebastian is martyred by the arrows of Cupid, but the honesty and purity of his songs enable them to survive the ironies of their framework.

"Genesis," one of Hill's earliest poems, can be seen in retrospect as foreshadowing his poetic development. Strife is implicit in nature from the moment of creation. The violence of nature and history is not as surprising as the presumptuousness of one who assumes that man can transcend the natural condition. The energies of thought and language, like those of nature, exist only in conflict; a reassuring idea is a dead idea that can only nourish an efflorescence belying its former truth. Yet one fact remains to be explained (if I read Hill's later work correctly)—the fact that will and desire cannot be appeased. Whether this fact can be embodied in poetry remains problematic in that when expressed (in language or action), will and desire are caught up in the foreordained conflict of existence. In literature, representation of something beyond language can be achieved only through rhetorical strategies, and on that frontier of art and consciousness much remains to be explored.

The assertion that the poetry of Hill grows directly out of the modern tradition is not intended to insure [him] some privileged status in relation to poets who have simply rejected modernism. Arnold's dictum that "the creation of a modern poet, to be worth much, implies a great critical effort behind it" does not state a sufficient condition for poetic achievement, and the work behind creation need not be apparent in the resultant artifact. But the continuities of tradition deserve at least as much attention as declarations of discontinuity. In discussing the poetry of Hill, I have emphasized conceptual themes and hope thereby to have shed light on the critical effort underlying his poetic development. What his poetry needs most is to be read, after which there will be a need for structural analysis that will disclose how he leads the reader from one revelation to the next. A new kind of poetry, one that does not attain to an all-embracing unity of symbolic meaning, requires a new kind of criticism. . . .

Hill's single vision has gradually turned on itself to question its very being. The process of questioning is mediated by superimposed personae or by history; its result can be endless reflection or startling, almost painful revelation. In his case a challenge to modernist assumptions about unity has led to new forms of creation.

JON SILKIN

The Poetry of Geoffrey Hill

The word "formal" in criticism often associates with ideas concerning metrical iambic, strict stanzaic form and rhyme, and the containment by these devices of whatever the poet has to say. It may be used approvingly, or, since the current has recently run more the other way, as a means of implying that a poet using these forms has little to say, and that his sensibility and imagination are insensitive, that the courage a poet needs in order to articulate what ought essentially to be his way of exploring life is absent. As corollary to this, it is implied that only what is new in structure can sensitively and honestly engage this, since, it is argued, we are in the midst of such changes that only those forms originated by the poet in co-operation with his constantly changing environment can adequately express the new (as well as the past and hidden) in the tormenting life so many are forced to live.

The second position is persuasive, providing one keeps in mind the counter-balancing caveat that every more-or-less defined position provides the grounds for much bad work; and that even if the second position seems to account for a greater share of low-tension poetry, it is arguable that the position has helped into existence poetry that might not otherwise have got written (*vide* Alvarez writing of Plath and citing Lowell). On the other hand one might ask what there is in such a position for Hill, whose work contrasts so strongly with, say, Ginsberg, and the Hughes of *Crow*.

There is, however, another way of defining "formal", which involves the origination of constraints and tensions with those forms themselves evolved by the concerns of the writer and his sensibility, as he or she

From *British Poetry Since 1960*, edited by Michael Schmidt and Grevel Lindop. Copyright © 1972 by Jon Silkin. Carcanet Press, Ltd.

worked these. One might say that a co-existing condition of the material evolving its forms involved, for this kind of formal writer, a productive impediment, a compacting of certain forms of speech, refracting the material into a mode of compression and close conjunction not normally found in speech, and which, probably, could not be found there. Such a definition, however, would imply that the mode of response, which could be brought to conscious active thought, was habitual to such a writer. The question of conjunction is especially important to such a poet as Hill, and in making these definitions, I have been trying to illustrate both a general type and identify a particular writer.

Such formality bears with its own problems. The payments on such a premium are continuous, and one way of apprehending this condition in Hill's work is to consider the variety of forms; to consider the restlessness within the variety. Formality of the first sort occurs with Hill's early poem "Genesis", although here it seems that the formal iambic line, stanza, and section, are used to *express* that already stylised conception of earth's creation; and that the formality while representing such stylisation is already at odds with the central theme of the poem

> There is no bloodless myth will hold

and to a lesser extent with the sub-theme's concession

> And by Christ's blood are men made free.

Hill's "argument with himself" over formal means and expressiveness is already embryonically visible in the poem, but, for the moment, one might consider the difference in form between say this poem (and "In memory of Jane Fraser"—a poem he has had trouble with) and "September Song"; between that, and the unrhymed sonnets of "Funeral Music" and between all these and the prose hymns (canticles) of *Mercian Hymns*.

Restlessness of forms is not something one would normally associate with Hill's work, but this is probably because the voice is unusually present and distinct. Sometimes it becomes over-distinctive, and this is usually the result of the formal means degenerating into mannerisms. Even so, a voice cannot itself provide more than a spurious unity, and to put on it work that is beyond its proper capacity produces the strain that exists in a fraction of Hill's work. This "mannered" and "mild humility", however, is more often disrupted by the variety of forms. Is it imaginative experimentation, or an inability to find one embracing and therefore controlling mode? It could be argued that such unity is undesirable, but I am suggesting that for a poet such as Hill, unity of form, as of thought and response, are important.

This is why we have such apparently absolute control within each poem (or form) but such variety of form over the spread of his work so far. Each fragment of absoluteness represents a pragmatic concession to the intractable nature of the matter and response to it in each poem. One is glad that it is so, and it reflects the ongoing struggle between form, expressiveness, and the scrupulous attention Hill usually gives to his material, even when it is struggling against that oppressive attention so as to return an existence (in life) independent of his own.

II

Hill's use of language, and choice of words, has been noticed, often, one feels, to the detriment of his themes. One sympathises with the reviewers. The compressed language is intimately bound up with what it is conveying. This is true of many poets, but true to an unusual degree with Hill. It is true in another sense. The language itself is unlike most other writing current, and coupled with this is an unusually self-conscious pointing on the part of the poet to the language. This is not because he wishes to draw attention to it for its own sake, but because the language both posits his concerns, and is itself, in the way it is used, an instance of them. Moreover, his use of language is both itself an instance of his (moral) concerns, and the sensuous gesture that defines them. It is therefore difficult to speak of his themes without coming first into necessary contact with the language.

Hill's use of irony is ubiquitous, but is not, usually, of the non-participatory and mandarin sort. It articulates the collision of events, or brings them together out of concern, and for this a more or less regular and simple use of syntax is needed, and used.

> Undesirable you may have been, untouchable
> you were not.

A concentration camp victim. Even the "play" in the subtitle "born 19.6.32—deported 24.9.42" where the natural event of birth is placed, simply, beside the human and murderous "deported" as if the latter were of the same order and inevitability for the victim; which, in some senses, it was—even here, the zeugmatic wit is fully employed. The irony of conjuncted meanings between "undesirable" (touching on both sexual desire and racism) and "untouchable", which exploits a similar ambiguity but reverses the emphases, is unusally dense *and* simple. The confrontation is direct and unavoidable, and this directness is brought to bear on the reader not only by the vocabulary, but by the balancing directness of the syntax.

This stanza contains one of Hill's dangerous words—dangerous because of its too-frequent use, and because these words sometimes unleash (though not here) a too evident irony:

> Not forgotten
> or passed over at the proper time.

"Proper" brings together the idea of bureaucratically correct "as calculated" by the logistics of the "final solution" and the particular camp's timetable; it also contrasts the idea of the mathematically "correct" with the morally intolerable. It touches, too, on the distinction between what is morally right, and what is conventionally acceptable, and incidentally brings to bear on the whole the way in which the conventionally acceptable is often used to cloak the morally unacceptable. One of Hill's grim jokes, deployed in such a way that the laughter is precisely proportionate to the needs of ironic exposure. It is when the irony is in excess of the situation that the wit becomes mannered. But here it does not. So the poem continues, remorselessly.

> As estimated, you died. Things marched,
> sufficient, to that end.

One feels the little quibbling movement in

> As estimated, you died

as, without wishing to verbalise it, Hill points to the disturbing contrast between the well-functioning time-table and what it achieved. "Things marched" has the tread of pompous authority, immediately, in the next line, qualified by the painfully accurate recognition that just so much energy was needed, and released, for the extermination. "Sufficient" implies economy, but it also implies a conscious qualification of the heavy, pompous tread of authority. The quiet function of unpretentious machinery fulfilled its programme, perhaps more lethally. One also notices here how the lineation gauges, exactly, the flow and retraction of meaning and impulse, and how this exact rhythmical flow is so much a part of the sensuous delivery of response and evaluation. It is speech articulated, but the lineation provides, via the convention of verse line-ending, a formal control of rhythm, and of sense emphasis, by locking with, or breaking, the syntactical flow. Thus in the third stanza the syntax is broken by the lineation exactly at those parts at which the confession, as it were, of the poem's (partial) source is most painful:

> (I have made
> an elegy for myself it
> is true)

The slightly awkward break after "it" not only forces the reading speed down to a word-by-word pace, in itself an approximation to the pain of the confession, but emphasises the whole idea. By placing emphasis on the unspecifying pronoun, Hill is able to say two things: that the elegy was made for himself (at least, in part) since in mourning another one is also commiserating with one's own condition.

> When we chant
> "Ora, ora pro nobis" it is not
> Seraphs who descend to pity but ourselves.

But "it" may also refer to the whole event; I have made an elegy for myself, as we all do, but I have also made an elegy on a "true" event. True imaginatively, true in detailed fact; both for someone other than myself. Thus he is able to point to the difficulty of the poet, who wishes, for a variety of reasons, to approach the monstrousness of such events, but has compunction about doing so. He tactfully touches for instance on the overweening ambition of the poet who hitches his talent to this powerful subject, thereby giving his work an impetus it *may* not be fully entitled to, since, only the victim, herself, would be entitled to derive this kind of "benefit". But he also modestly pleads, I think, with "it/is true" that whatever the reasons for his writing such an elegy, a proper regard for the victim, a true and unambitious feeling, was present and used. I hope enough has been said here to point to Hill's use of irony at its best, and to indicate that the tact with which he uses language is not a convention of manners which he is inertly content to remain immersed in, but an active employment of the convention as it co-operates with his scrupulousness. The scrupulousness, like the pity, is in the language. The theme permeates it.

III

In pointing to the importance of the Imagist movement as it has affected English and American poetry, one is of course considering how central the image has become both in the writing, and for the considering, of twentieth-century poetry. What is strange about this is that apparently unrelated movements and poets apparently ignorant of each other were writing in modes which had certain formal elements in common. The hermetic poems of Ungaretti's earlier period as well as certain of Pound's and Eliot's earlier poems use the hard, clear image, seemingly as an instrument considered valuable for its own sake. In the expressionist poetry of Stramm, the images are used, as Michael Hamburger has indicated, as the only needful flesh of the poem; the poem disdains the use of syntactical connections, thereby placing upon the image the whole burden of expressive meaning and impulse. To a lesser extent one finds this preoccupation with the image in Lorca; although even here one feels that sometimes the syntactical connections are used to lay stress on the image thereby placing on it a similar labour. The image becomes that point at which an ignition of all the elements of meaning and response takes place; that is, not only do the meanings and their impulses get expressed, but at that point are given their principal impetus. Even with the hard clear image calmly delivered this occurs. Hill has been both the innocent partaker and victim in this. He has used and been used. This is partly because of course the age as it were reeks of such practice. But with Hill one also feels that the choice has been made because he has come to recognise that the use of the image can properly communicate the intensity he wishes to express. Through it he can express the intensity, but fix it in such a way that it will evaluate the concerns of the poem it is embedded in without its intensity overruling the other parts. The intensity finds in its own kind of formality its own controlling expression. At the same time, the image as artefact has a perhaps satisfactory and not unmodest existence. It can be regarded, but it is also useful. Curiously enough, although the impression of imagery in Hill is, in my mind at least, strong, checking through the poetry, one is surprised at how controlled is the frequency of the kind of imagery I am thinking of. There are many instances of images used to represent objects, creatures, events. But it is as though the image whereby one object is enriched by the verbal presence of another, combined with it, and a third thing made— as though such a creation were recognised as so potentially powerful, and so open to abuse, that he was especially careful to use it sparingly. And he is, rightly, suspicious of offering confection to readers who enjoy the local richness without taking to them the full meaning of the poem, which is only susceptible to patience and a care for what it is as a whole thing. He says as much:

> Anguish bloated by the replete scream. . . .
>   I could cry "Death! Death!" as though
> To exacerbate that suave power;
>
> But refrain. For I am circumspect,
> Lifting the spicy lid of my tact
> To sniff at the myrrh.

The images have a richness, but here he is not so much reproaching himself for that, although he implies such a possibility, but rather for the perhaps evasive caution which is characterised by "tact". The self-questioning exposes further recessions of self-doubts and questions, themselves seen to be faintly absurd. There are other examples, however, of the kind of image I am describing:

> Bland vistas milky with Jehovah's calm—

and

>   cleanly
>   maggots churning spleen
> to milk

from a poem for another concentration camp victim, Robert Desnos; and

>   we are dying
> to satisfy fat Caritas, those
> Wiped jaws of stone

and from the earlier Dr. Faustus:

> A way of many ways: a god
> Spirals in the pure steam of blood.

What is noticeable about these images, chosen for the way in which they combine disparate elements, is their ferocity. Their expressiveness occurs at its fullest in the moment of sudden expansion, when the elements combine in often intolerable antipathy and produce judgements issuing from a disgust that has behind it a sense of outrage at this or that situation.

More often the images are "abstract", combinations of adjectives and nouns, whose conjunction is ironically disruptive, but with a similar moral evaluation intended. Thus in one of Hill's best shorter poems, "Ovid in the Third Reich", we again confront his justly obsessive concern with innocence, and its mutilation, or impossibility, within the context of human barbarism:

> Too near the ancient troughs of blood
> Innocence is no earthly weapon.

The notion of innocence as a defence against earthly corruption has an ancient lineage; but here it is linked with the more combative "weapon", and in such a way as to suggest weapon in a very literal sense. Of what use is innocence in such a context? And: if it is of no use on earth, what is its use? Are we right to think of a condition as useless because inoperative on earth? And if thus inoperative, can it be so valued in a "heavenly" context? Hovering near the phrase "earthly weapon" is the phrase (no) "earthly good" with its worn-through substance, a little restored by Hill's regenerative irony. In these two lines Hill returns of course to the consideration of "Genesis"

> There is no bloodless myth will hold.

(The "Ovid" poem suggests *to me* an Eichmann-like figure—not Eichmann—with whom the reader in his ordinariness and banality is invited to identify, thus being asked to make the connection with that other aspect of Eichmann, his evil. Ovid's exile may be seen to parallel our inability, or reluctance, to associate with guilt—in case we sully an innocence—already sullied.)

There are many examples of these "abstract" combinations, often zeugmatic in form (the device which has built into it a moral judgement). Thus

> fastidious trumpets
> Shrilling into the ruck

and

> my justice, wounds, love
> Derisive light, bread, filth

and, at the funeral of King Offa, the punning zeugma where the successive adjective suffers qualification by the former:

> He was defunct. They were perfunctory.

And again from *Mercian Hymns*, the man who has imagined, with ambiguous relish, a scene of torture

> wiped his lips and hands. He strolled back to the
> car, with discreet souvenirs for consolation. . . .

"Discreet" is not an image precisely, but it produces an image of a man hiddenly guilty, voyeur upon his own imagination, which is, however, discreet in that it is secret. It has not tortured another's flesh.

In these instances, where Hill's intensity is released, I have tried to show that it is through images, of several kinds, that the sudden evaluative expansion occurs. Hill has more recently been concerned to accumulate meaning and response in a more gradual way. But, in the earlier work especially, the intense evaluation, response, judgement—all are released at that sudden moment of expansion which is the moment of visualisation. Hill's poetry has more often consisted of, not continuous narrative, but a conjunction of imagistic impulses. A conjunction of intensities, sometimes sensuously rich, and nearly always scrupulously evaluative.

IV

The imagistic impulsion in Hill's work, as both imagistic and image-making, is of course related to the question of narrative and discursiveness. Imagism, considered as a reaction, developed out of an antipathy for the discursive nature of Victorian poetry. That was not the sum of its antipathies, but it is clear, from the principles and the practice, that Imagism constituted, among other things, an attempt to enact, rather than assert, a response. It wanted to cut from it those dilutions of response which had rendered a verse that was vaguely descriptive of states of feelings, and it found a method. It found in the image a pure answer. That is, it found in the image something that could not be adulterated. An image did not attempt to explain; it rendered the verbal equivalent of what was seen, and the more it rendered exactly what it saw, the better. Clearly this kind of antidote was needed in English poetry and we are still receiving its benefits. Yet the difficulty lay in that by nature, the hard, clear image, untroubled by a discursive reflectiveness, had little or no valency. It could only accommodate other images, perhaps of different intensities and implications, and it could not accommodate the syntax of argument or narrative. And despite what its claims implied, it could hardly accommodate connections of any kind; Imagism had to select very carefully indeed, and its methods could not easily be used without its being diluted. And at that stage in its development, to dilute its purity would have been to have annulled its impetus. What it gained in intensity it lost in its capacity to cope with a range of experience.

This is immediately apparent when we consider Imagism in relation to the war. This is not the place to speak in detail of, for instance, Aldington and Herbert Read, but, briefly, I should like to instance two very different poems by Read—"The Happy Warrior" and "The End of a War". In the first, Read manages to make of his war experience an imagist poem. That is, he manages to make the "syntax" of Imagism render a particular set of very careful responses to combat, and to render, by implication, a set of arguments. But this is one instance, which, once done, could not be repeated. Moreover, the poem relies, for its deepest reading, on its being correlated with Wordsworth's poem "The Character of the Happy Warrior" of which it is also a criticism. But the fact that it needs, finally, this correlation with a poem that is anything but imagistic places Read's poem in a special relation to Imagism. Nothing like this that I know of in Imagist poetry had been done before, and one suspects that Read found his necessities out of what he called war's "terrorful and inhuman events".

In his autobiography, *The Contrary Experience*, Read wrote:

I criticised [the Imagists] because in their manifestoes they had renounced the decorative word, but their sea-violets and wild hyacinths tend to become as decorative as the beryls and jades of Oscar Wilde. I also accused them of lacking that aesthetic selection which is the artist's most peculiar duty. . . . We were trying to maintain an abstract aesthetic ideal in the midst of terrorful and inhuman events.

There is of course a skeletal narrative structure in "The Happy Warrior" but poems could hardly be written like that of any length and complexity. In his subsequent "war poems", those composing *Naked Warriors* (1919), we see Read introducing narrative, but the imagistic elements are much diluted by it, and in such a way as to enervate the poetry. In other words, Read had relied, as he had to, upon the imagistic elements to render intensity and expressiveness, but the collision of the two modes produced compromise. By the time Read came to write *The End of a War* (published 1933) he had worked out a solution; he pushed the narrative outside the poem, setting the scene and describing the events of the episode in a prefacing prose argument which, though essential to the reading of the poem, is in ambiguous relationship to it, and without any relationship to it structurally.

Hill is clearly a poet having little in common with Read, but he has, I think, similar problems engaging him. "Genesis" for instance is held together by using days of the week as a means of tabulating impulsions in sequence. The sequence of days is important to the poem structurally, and through it Hill tries to initiate an image of growing consciousness. Yet is only a proper sequence as it refers back to God's six days of work. The poem itself does not have narrative coherence so much as a sequence of formulisations; in his subsequent work, Hill abandoned this kind of stylisation, and to a lesser extent, the incipient narrative structure.

With "Funeral Music", the prose note that at one time preceded the poem stands in similar elucidatory relation to it as Read's "Argument" does to "The End of a War". Less, perhaps, or perhaps less in Hill's mind, for the note has, in *King Log* itself, been placed at the end of the book, and separate from the poems, as though Hill were determined, with such a gesture, to make "Funeral Music" un-needful of any elucidatory material. The poems do not form a narrative sequence, although they lead through the battle (of Towton) into some deliberately incomplete attempts at evaluating the cost in both physical and spiritual excoriation. Evaluation is made partly by reference to a supposed, or possibly supposed, after-life, in which the ideals of an exemplary spiritual life would if anywhere be found; partly by reference to this, or to eternity, yet into which no sense of human evaluation can be extended with the certainty of finding corroborative "echoes". (Compare the following with the first stanza of "Ovid in the Third Reich".)

> If it is without
> Consequence when we vaunt and suffer, or
> If it is not, all echoes are the same
> In such eternity. Then tell me, love,
> How that should comfort us—

Even supposed *notions* of an after-life, with its spiritual absolutes, are insufficient here since the first of the unrhymed sonnets opens in platonic supposition; that is, the platonic structure throws into ambiguity the question of whether we are to suppose an after-life is to be believed in—does this by supplanting the idea of an after-life with its own metaphysical scheme. I am indicating here that in Hill's longer poems, sequences and extended work that demand some correspondingly developed structure, he meets the problem without conceding to narrative a function it might usefully fulfil in his work. Fearful of sacrificing the imagistic purity of his work, of sullying that compression, of impairing a dramatic enactment, or mimesis of psychological impulses, he prefers to accumulate intensities than involve them in accumulating and continuous action. This may partly be due to the preference Hill shows for writing that, by dramatic mimesis, introduces to the reader internal impulses rather than dramatic action. Thus in "Funeral Music", the battle of Towton, and its murderousness, is not encapsulated as dramatic action, but brooded on after the event, thereby allowing the external state of the field and the state of the mind experiencing and responding to it to meet. It is the self-questioning, the doubts, the beliefs half-held with a conviction of personal honesty, the motives and the state of the spirit, that interest Hill, rather than the shaping action of narrative. Nevertheless, these things too have their form of collision with other minds, and through action, alter and are altered. And they could also, I feel, build a narrative unity that Hill has only tentatively, if at all, used.

One of the most interesting and moving aspects of "Funeral Music" is its plainness. The images in the following passage do not fabricate either a local richness to colour-up the passage, nor is there an over-arching image employed supposedly to enlarge or make more significant the events and the responses to these of the observer-participant:

> "At noon,
> As the armies met, each mirrored the other;
> Neither was outshone. So they flashed and vanished
> And all that survived them was the stark ground
> Of this pain. I made no sound, but once
> I stiffened as though a remote cry
> Had heralded my name. It was nothing . . ."
> Reddish ice tinged the reeds; dislodged, a few
> Feathers drifted across; carrion birds
> Strutted upon the armour of the dead.

An Ecclesiastes-like consideration of vanity moves in these first lines, located in the ironic flashing of the armies mirrored in each other's armour. But they do not see themselves; they see only the flash of their *own* pride by which they are, each of them, dazzled. Yet with an honesty that compels a grudging kind of admission, we are also told that theirs was a kind of sad "glory": "Neither was outshone". But this is also qualified by the other idea inherent in the phrase—that neither had more pride, nor was more capable of victory; what is impending is not the surfeiting of pride but its extinction in the futility of combat. If they mirror each other's pride they also mirror each other's destruction. The strutting carrion birds confirm this judgement.

Yet impressive as this is as narration implicated with judgement, and pity, there is also a turning inwards and sealing off from the outward visible of all this in the ambiguous "the stark ground/Of this pain". The ground is at once the actual ground where soldiers inflicted pain on each other; it is also, because of the disposition of the syntax, a kind of personification where the ground itself becomes absorbed in the huge lingering tremor of pain. This serves to incarcerate the reader, and perhaps the writer also, in an inescapable response, but it also fails, I think, to release him from a pre-occupation where the event has been so internalised that there results more response than event itself. The passage seems to recognise this by resuming its re-creation of the desolate battlefield. The sense of the pentameter, in these lines, and throughout the sequence, serves not merely a unifying function but as a framework within and around which Hill can make his supple impulses and retractions of rhythm:

> ". . . as though a remote cry
> Had heralded my name. It was nothing . . ."
> Reddish ice tinged the reeds; dislodged, a few
> Feathers drifted across.

The second line begins with a slow, regular pentameter; after the word "name", the expectations of the pentameter are reduced in the foreshortened remainder of the line, reducing exactly the expectations of the person in the *poem* as his feelings are disappointed. In the next line the pentameter is extended. The other speaking voice is describing minute events on the surface of the battle-field. "Dislodged", in its participial form, is syntactically isolated, and mirrors the disconnectedness of the feathers, from a bird, or some martial plume, but reflects also the disconnectedness of the dead from the living. In the little halting movement at the end of the line, which the line-break emphasises, the temporary emphasis falls on "few" and thus serves to re-create sensuously the stillness of the battle-field which is

> its own sound
> Which is like nothing on earth, but is earth.

These lines, from No. 3 of the sequence, serve to pre-resonate the irony of the situation, where the dead are unearthly (because of the possibility of the dead having an after-life) but are for us no more than the earth they have been reduced to by human action. Seen in this way, "Funeral Music" is, among other things, a consideration of war where "war", to use Clausewitz's strategy "is a continuation of state policy by other means". The sequence is at once an elegy of pity, an examination of pride, a self-examination of the responses appropriate to this apparent constant in human living. It is all these in relation to the question of whether suffering has any meaning in earthly life; and whether there exists some ideal platonic and/or spiritual system in which suffering, which is perhaps the only state during which we are innocent, can have a meaningful and positive place.

V

Sebastian Arrurruz ("The Songbook of Sebastian Arrurruz") was, as we now know, not an actual poet (1868–1922) who has bewilderedly survived into the twentieth century, but an invention that may have perplexed critics searching for the original work.

The poem makes use of the necessary "silence" surrounding the "original". The lack of information on the poet may obliquely refer to Arrurruz's own apprehension regarding the oblivion both of himself and his work, and is thus a wry part of the poems themselves. The poems composed by Arrurruz are also records of certain attitudes towards both the (discontinued) relationship with his mistress and to poetry. In a sense the poem, or group, is Hill's *Mauberley*. But where Pound is using himself, both for what he feels himself to be kin to as a poet, and for what the figure stands in contradistinction to in the effete and vulgar English culture, Hill's

Sebastian (the saint pierced with arrows) is more separate from the poet who has shaped him.

Arrurruz (arrowroot) is a man pierced by the arrow (another's predation upon his relinquished mistress); the arrow remains rooted in him. He is also a man, the root of an arrow, himself equipped, organically, and with the incising gift of the poet. Both these, though, in the poem, are laconically expressed, and survive increasingly on the wryly self-regretful memory of what once obtained. But this double image, of potency, and the quite powerful if intermittent observation of it, serves to illustrate, among other things, the fate of The Poet surviving through two eras. The original potency may have had a bardic vigour unimpeded by a self-conscious and mocking observation of its impulsions; but the later work of Arrurruz that we are offered presents a considerable shift in temper and emphasis. In these poems we have, initially, not so much a man expressing passion as recollecting it:

> Ten years without you. For so it happens. . . .
>
> The long-lost words of choice and valediction.

The energy is not in the passion itself, but re-located in the stare that recollects it, and which is itself observed. Arrurruz's writing is at once more complex than it was, and, significantly, more difficult to achieve. Whatever the auto-biographical references may amount to, Hill is clearly defining the poet's difficulties as he encounters an environment that is at once more self-conscious and less bardic. The attention is scrupulous and modern.

Arrurruz is of course a middle-ageing man, and knows it. Yet his struggles are not those of a defeated one.

> "One cannot lose what one has not possessed."
> So much for that abrasive gem.
> I can lose what I want. I want you.

The first line is between inverted commas because it is a line from a poem he is writing or has perhaps recently completed. Either way the line is embedded in commentary by an older, more self-conscious, part of the man. "Coplas"—this is the first of four that constitute the poem—are "songs", perhaps somewhat lyrically un-selfregarding and unironic poems. They are also popular poems, often used to serenade the beloved. Some measure of Hill's irony here may be obtained by contrasting these simple definitions with the stance of the present Arrurruz's coplas which form neither a serenade, nor are popular, but unlyrical, allusive, and complex. The form is of course traditional and it has therefore accumulated to itself the energy of those poems which have earlier filled the form. But like so much else in the twentieth century, the traditional form has broken down. Or rather, not so much broken as become inappropriate; and not this, entirely, but that we have lost the ability to use the form. We have lost spontaneity.

Much of this centres in the phrase "abrasive gem". It is abrasive because it is a reminder of what he has lost. It is a gem because it is a lyrical utterance faceted and cut like a jewel. Hill however uses "gem" to bring in other, colloquial meanings. Thus gem can mean a real beauty, but the poet can also, and certainly here does, mean it ironically and self-contemptuously. The self-contempt arises not only from his awareness of having lost his wife to another, but also of how his line of poetry untruthfully renders in lyrical terms a considerably unlyrical event. Arrurruz brings to his and our awareness the discontinuity between the two ways of looking at such an event, and the two ways of writing about it. There is no elegising or consolatory sweetness to be got; the paradox of Arrurruz's poem is still-born; and is replaced by the unparadoxical and unironical lack of conso-lation:

> I can lose what I want. I want you.

But in the second of the coplas there is already a modification of the harsh tone:

> Oh my dear one, I shall grieve for you
> For the rest of my life with slightly
> Varying cadence, oh my dear one.

The tone of this first line softens that of the previous copla's ending. He is, it seems, back in the convention of elegising the lost one. But the phrase "with slightly/varying cadence" tinges the whole with mockery. Is the irony conscious on Arrurruz's part, or is it reserved for the reader's inspection only? It hardly matters. The absurd monotony of such poetics is rendered, and we understand how the irony qualifies into clarity the whole situation. He is perhaps even beginning to write a poetry that feeds on such ironic awareness. Yet the irony cannot dissolve the passion, a crucial point for the poems that follow: "Half-mocking the half-truth." Michael Hamburger wrote of Hölderlin in *Reason and Energy*:

Even before his enforced separation from Susette Gontard he had felt that his fate would be a tragic one. . . . Now he was to lose his last support against the sense of personal tragedy. As he had foretold in 1798, all that remained was his art and the quite impersonal faith that sustained his art.

. . . What Hölderlin did not know when he wrote this poem is that long after his heart had indeed died, as he says, his "mellow song" would continue; that the music of his strings *would* escort him down.

So with Arrurruz, in a way. Abandoned by his wife, musing with increasing, dilapidating irony on his loss, seeing that the earlier way of writing will fit neither the age, nor the event in his life, nor now his temperament, nothing it seems can prevent his gentle decline into oblivion. One might therefore expect the poems to degenerate, by mimesis, placing at the reader's disposal an irreversible picture of disintegration, among a flickering irony. This does not occur. What Arrurruz could not have foreseen, since he was engaged in it, was that his ironically truthful examination of the events in his life, including his poetry, would revitalise his art. For I take it that the succeeding poems of the "Songbook" are not only made of Arrurruz speaking but of his writing. If so, there is no failure, but rather, regeneration. In poem 5, Arrurruz can respond to, or write, a poem of genuine deprivation:

> I find myself
> Devouring verses of stranger passion
> And exile. The exact words
> Are fed into my blank hunger for you.

A hunger that may not be fed; therefore blank. The crucial word, however, for the poet is "exact". The gaze has caught its truth. The reward is exactness, and its pain. Similarly in "A Song from Armenia":

> Why do I have to relive, even now,
> Your mouth, and your hand running over me
> Deft as a lizard, like a sinew of water?

The emphatic, simplified movement of the song has returned, but this time filled with rich, *painful* memories, constantly reawakened, and admitted into his consciousness by the wry ironic truthfulness with which the mind regards such experience. It is not the distancing irony of the man who can afford irony because he is detached, but an irony created in pain. The relationship may have ceased, but the pain does not get subsumed in distance. There are two final twists to the "life", both occurring in the second of the prose poems which conclude the sequence:

> Scarcely speaking: it becomes as a
> Coolness between neighbours. Often
> There is this orgy of sleep. I wake
> To caress propriety with odd words
> And enjoy abstinence in a vocation
> Of now-almost-meaningless despair.

"Orgy of sleep" oddly reverses the ironic vitality I have noticed, suggesting a dying inwards of life. The sexuality gets transcribed in a caressed "propriety". Yet the last word is despair. The registration is in the end one of feeling. Is there a further irony in that Arrurruz, caught up with an exact sense of it, can no longer make poems out of his pain because his equipment belongs to an earlier more rhetorical mode? I think not; although one can imagine that for Arrurruz this might often seem to have been the threat. As a latter-day saint, he experiences two temptations. One is to succumb to his earlier inexact rhetoric, as both an expression of and a response to his experience. The other is to create a distant and neutered irony from his pain. This latter gets suggested in "Postures". As it happens, Arrurruz succumbs to neither temptation.

VI

As with the Arrurruz sequence, the thirty prose poems that make up *Mercian Hymns* have a central figure from whom the poems depend, in this instance King Offa. Historically, as Hill tells us, Offa reigned over Mercia . . . in the years A.D. 757–796. During earlier medieval times he was already becoming a creature of legend. However the gloss is not entirely helpful in that the reader does not find a historical reconstruction of the King and his domain. Interleaved with a reconstruction of some of the King's acts are passages and whole poems concerned with the contemporary and representative figure Hill makes of himself. Why not? Additionally, the poem deliberately thwarts any attempts by the reader to keep his or her imagination safe in the past. The King himself, although rooted in the past, is to be "most usefully . . . regarded as the presiding genius of the West Midlands", and thus threads "his" way in and out of his past and our present. Hill makes quite sure we get this by offering, in the first Hymn, a description of the figure as

> King of the perennial holly-groves, the riven sand-
>   stone: overlord of the M5: architect of the his-
>   toric rampart and ditch. . . .

Nevertheless the historic facts of Offa the King are relevant, if tangled, and we should look at them. Entangled with them, however, are Hill's references themselves: (i) *Sweet's Anglo-Saxon Reader* and (ii) The Latin prose hymns or canticles of the early Christian Church; *The Penguin Book of Latin Verse*.

The interested reader will not be glad to discover that although there is a group of Hymns in Anglo-Saxon, quoted by Sweet, these texts are interlineally placed with the Latin taken from the *Vulgate*, of which these are literal and apparently not always accurate translations. Moreover it has been suggested that these translations embody no sense of the haecceity of the Mercian domain, or of the Anglo-Saxon world at large. That is, they were probably intended as instructional texts for the teaching of Latin. Moreover the two Vulgates are themselves of course translations from the Hebrew, the relevant Biblical references being made by Sweet at the head of each Anglo-Saxon translation (from the Latin). The first reference then suggests that, apart from some elaborate, heavy-witted joke, Hill's pointing to the Mercian Hymns indicates no more, as far as the Anglo-Saxon is concerned, than a homogeneity sanctioned by the Mercian dialect, a homogeneity that stems of course from a geographical area over which King Offa did rule, whose reign may or may not have witnessed these translations.

The second reference is as apparently oblique: "The 'Te Deum', a canticle in rhythmical prose, has been used in Christian worship from the fourth century to the present day. . . . As the Jewish psalter was the sole hymnbook of the early Church, it is not surprising that the 'Te Deum' is characterised throughout by the parallelism which is the basis of ancient Hebrew poetry." As it happens, there appears to be no use of Hebrew parallelism in Hill's poems other than those traces which, through contact with the Bible, have crept into our speech and left there residually a few emphatic forms. Yet checking, in fact, through the relevant Biblical passages in Isaiah, Deuteronomy, Habakkuk, and Luke (which are the original texts for Sweet's Mercian Hymns) I found, almost by accident, and by linking my apprehension of rhythm in these English passages with the phrase quoted earlier—the "Te Deum", a canticle in rhythmical prose—I began to follow the point of the references, and even to give grudging assent to their obliquity.

It is helpful to remember that much of the *Old Testament* is, in the Hebrew, poetry, and that in rendering these translations in English of the Authorised Version, what is offered us is, precisely, "rhythmical prose". Moreover it is not merely rhythmical prose, but prose versions of poetry, although rendered, one feels, partly through the repetitions of parallelism, with emphatic *and* subtle rhythms. It is as if the exterior device of line ending, and all those devices contingent on this convention, have been discarded (not *entirely* true of *Mercian Hymns*); what is left, in the main, however, is the inherent structure itself, depending more than ever upon the rhythmical arrangement of the words. Greater stress may get laid on word-choice, and a closer attention is charged, perhaps, upon the meaning. These hopeful attempts at describing a prose poem, but in particular Hill's canticles, now offer the point of the references, since, without falling back on a description of his own method of writing, they allow the reader to pick up, in the best possible way, through example, the kind of poetry he is writing in *Mercian Hymns.* Moreover, although the Mercian dialect and the Anglo-Saxon language have little to do with the structure of the Hymns, and no comparison with the Anglo-Saxon will profitably help us in a reading of Hill's poems, I suggest that the Anglo-Saxon *Mercian Hymns* act as a historical filter for Hill. That is, they remind us that the Biblical trans-missions which reach us additionally passed, for whatever reason, through the Mercian dialect, and that however indistinct the locality is now, and however restricted King Offa's jurisdiction may have been, Biblical contact was made via Mercia, which is also Offa's and Hill's locality.

As for the relevance of the Bible to King Offa, and both these to the character of Offa in Hill's poems, verse 21 from *Deuteronomy* 32 may help:

> They have moved me to jealousy with that which is not God; they have provoked me to anger with their vanities: and I will move them to jealousy with those which are not a people; I will provoke them to anger with a foolish nation.

In Hill's eighth poem:

> The mad are predators. Too often lately they harbour
> against us. A novel heresy exculpates all maimed
> souls. Abjure it! I am the King of Mercia, and
> I know. . . .
>
> Today I name them; tomorrow I shall express the new
> law. I dedicate my awakening to this matter.

It is useful to remember that while all of chapter 32 of *Deuteronomy* consists of God's words, Moses speaks them. They have the backing of God, but are vested in Moses' temporal authority. Of course, Moses the prime leader of Israel in a tight situation, had much to cope with, not least of all the comically frequent backsliding of the Israelites. But we recall that Moses was an autocratic ruler and, in this, had adequate sanction from the God of the *Old Testament,* who was jealous and wrathful. Curiously, those pas-sages of the Bible translated into Anglo-Saxon stress, perhaps by accident, this aspect of God: provided we obey Him we shall find Him loving and protective: but should we not, we shall discover his wrath and punishments. The autocratic nature of such a God was perhaps a useful reminder, in that probably more anarchic period, that the nature and power of the Anglo-Saxon King was not unlike that of the Hebrew God.

R. W. Chambers in *Beowulf: an Introduction* interestingly examines the character of King Offa II as well as the legends surrounding his supposed ancestor Offa I. He points to the shuffling of the deeds of the King onto his Queen by the monks of St. Alban's as a way of exonerating their benefactor of crime. Chambers speaks explicitly of "the deeds of murder which, as a matter of history, did characterise [King Offa II's] reign". History helps us to link the autocratic nature of God with King Offa, and see too what Hill has done with this in his *Mercian Hymns.*

Finally, I should quote from C. H. Sisson's Epigraph for *Mercian Hymns:*

> The conduct of government rests upon the same foundation and encoun-
> ters the same difficulties as the conduct of private persons.

The quotation goes on to suggest that the technical aspects of government are frequently used to evade those moral laws which apply alike to individuals and governments.

The question of the private man and his public actions is one that Hill has already worked in "Ovid in the Third Reich". With such a figure as a king the question multiplies in direct ratio to the power of the king and his abuse of it. History suggests that Offa was a tyrant. In No. 7 ("The Kingdom of Offa"), a part of Offa's childhood, we have

> Ceolred was his friend and remained so, even after
>   the day of the lost fighter. . . .
>   Ceolred let it spin through a hole
> in the classroom-floorboards. . . .
> After school he lured Ceolred, who was sniggering
>   with fright, down to the old quarries, and flayed him.

Then he continues with his play, alone. One cannot mistake the ferocity, or the egocentric peace of mind following it. Hill does not set out to establish the figure of a tyrant, since the sequence does not have that kind of narrative structure or intention. Yet in Offa's adult life the poems produce a similar ruthlessness to that of the child. Thus in dealing (in No. 11) with forgers of the realm's coinage:

> [the King's "moneyers"] struck with account-
>   able tact. They could alter the king's face.
>
> Exactness of design to deter imitation; mutil-
>   ation if that failed. . . .
>
> Swathed bodies in the long ditch; one eye upstaring.
>   It is safe to presume, here, the king's anger.

"Safe" underlies the irony and helps us to refer back to his "moneyers" who, alone, were free to alter, that is, flatter, the face. One is reminded of the monks rewriting the *Life* of King Offa their benefactor, by putting on his Queen the murder of his vassal, King Aethelbert. But the flattery tactfully (via Hill) points to the King's severity, if not cruelty. Of course we see here the attempt to establish in the kingdom the idea of money available only through productive work, and an attempt to establish a concept of lawfulness. Yet one is also aware of the naked word "moneyers", as opposed to the more neutral words available, with the suggestion that the King is, out of "good substance", making money. There are many qualifications here, and if the judgement is finally against Offa in the poem, there are mitigations. In poem 14, Offa assumes the role of powerful businessman:

> Dismissing reports and men, he put pressure on the
> wax, blistered it to a crest. He threatened male-
> factors with ash from his noon cigar.

The effect is one of humour, and opulence. The ritual "noon" cigar suggests the power of a minor potentate. The power has its reserves; yet in the obvious sense the vulgarity is miniature; he threatens with "ash". But ash, we recall, is what the concentration camp victims were reduced to. One notices the zeugma, with the built-in moral device. Men are dismissed as easily and thoughtlessly as reports (the line-split, male/factor, emphasises this by means of the pun). The touch is light and has humour; but it engages the reader only to repel him.

There are other touches of opulence, of a more private kind, connected even more with the contemporary man than the king. He has been driving (in No. 17) through the beautiful "hushed Vosges". Some accident occurs with or between cyclists. It is unclear to me if it involves himself, as an adult, with these cyclists, or himself as a child with another cyclist, or whether Hill is merging both possibilities. In a sense it hardly matters. What is more important is the implied lack of compunction, whoever was to blame for the accident. The car "heartlessly" overtakes all this and

> He lavished on
> the high valleys its *haleine*.

By using, it would seem, the more delicate if exotic French for "breath", Hill is able to draw attention to the discrepancy between the beauty of the country he travels through, and the linked "heartlessness" of the pollution and lack of concern for the accident. The French word is beautiful, but cold, and lacks compunction in its erasure of concern.

Again in No. 18, we return to the problems of cruelty, with the contingent problem of the enjoyment of it:

> At Pavia, a visitation of some sorrow. Boethius'
> dungeon. He shut his eyes. . . .
>   He willed the instruments of
> violence to break upon his meditation. Iron buckles
> gagged; flesh leaked rennet over them; the men
> stooped, disentangled the body.
>
> He wiped his lips and hands. He strolled back to the
> car, with discreet souvenirs for consolation and
> philosophy.

The irony emerges. Boethius wrote his *De Consolatione Philosophiae* while imprisoned at Pavia. Still the tourist of the previous poem, the man visits Pavia with the conscious, formal intention of commiserating with Boethius' obscene death, and of wondering at the man who could console himself with philosophy at such a stage in his life. He wills himself to imagine the philosopher tortured, perhaps out of a dutiful compunction, but finds that, secretly, a part of him relishes the scene. "He wiped his lips and his hands". Both relish and guilt are here. The souvenirs are discreet because secret. He practises his enjoyment on no man's flesh. Yet there is a sense in which he is guilty, certainly, of unclean thoughts. The contrast between the cerebral and touristic appreciation of philosophy, and the voyeur's appreciation of cruelty is notable. Rather, he is not only voyeur, but, in his relish, participator. "Flesh leaked rennet over them" is horrifying; the blood curdles under the extremity of the suffering; the blood is said to leak, uncontrollably, as if itself incontinent. The wracked body becomes truly pitiful. The buckles restrain the victim, and perhaps muffle his cries; they also choke. What is remarkable here, however, is that the scene and its relishing are admitted to. Admitted to, but hardly confessed. It is not so much a release from guilt as a judgement on the thought and its stimulation. And this judgement is as valid for the tourist as for the king:

> I have learned one thing: not to look down
> So much upon the damned.

One should be careful to avoid the impression that there is relish in Hill's re-creation of cruelty. The pity is not punctured carelessly over the Hymns, as some kind of reward to the reader, but it is present, and, in particular, in the finely intimate and tender No. 25:

> I speak this in memory of my grandmother, whose
> childhood and prime womanhood were spent in the
> nailer's darg.

And

> It is one
> thing to celebrate the "quick forge", another
> to cradle a face hare-lipped by the searing wire.

The insight is crucial to the tender pity. It is one thing to celebrate the dignity of labour, another to endure it in one's first maturity, especially when the work itself has caused the mutilation. Even the sound of the phrase "nailer's darg", the phrase isolated on a line of its own and following a rather rapid syllabic flow—the long-drawn vowel of "darg" expresses the reductive nature of the experience. The poem does not indulge in melancholy. It consistently touches on the harshness of the experience. The man is said to "brood" on Ruskin's text concerning labour. Ruskin's letter, which begins with reflections on a Worchestershire nail factory, is concerned with the immorality and hypocrisy of usury. Hill is suggesting, I imagine, that his grandmother's labour, with that of others, borrows money from her employer, and his profit on that represents his interest.

One has to finish. Offa dies and one is left with not so much the figure of a man, but an area, changing, and filled, on balance, with more distress than comfort, and "presided over" by a ruler and an ethos more cruel, more harsh, than severely just. Capricious, light, but capable of some consistent authority. One may feel that the work as a whole is perhaps too inconclusive. On the other hand, as Lawrence abjured the novelist, Hill finally refuses to tip the balance by putting his own thumb on the scales. He is concerned with how things are (and an evaluation of that), not firstly upon how they ought to be; although that perhaps also emerges.

Number 27 is not the last of the Hymns but I should like to indicate its diverse elements, and to suggest how the entire set of poems, as they draw to their end, contrive to echo their diversity within this one poem. At the funeral of King Offa an absurd composition of mourners, from all ages, attends:

> He was defunct. They were perfunctory.

The contrast is not only between the finality of death and the continuity of the living. There is an absurdity contingent on death, but this is not entirely it either. The comic element here mediates between the two and both eases and recognises the sharpness of the dividing line. Additionally, as Hill suggests, the more public and dignified the man who has died, the more absurd the situation, and the more susceptible to hypocrisy, since those intimate, mourning connections, do not, properly, exist. The pun joins the living recognitions with the dead man, only to distinguish finally, and for good. Then follows a last stanza of extraordinary beauty, in which nature mirrors the uprooting of the man. But even in the largeness of the event, death is seen to touch every creature. It is the leveller:

> Earth lay for a while, the ghost-bride of livid
> Thor, butcher of strawberries, and the shire-tree
> dripped red in the arena of its uprooting.

"Butcher of strawberries" carries the right amount of pathos. The innocent fruits are remarked on.

STEPHEN UTZ

The Realism of Geoffrey Hill

In any literary work about people of the present in their relation to each other, there tends to arise what Lukács called "an abstract polarity of the eccentric and the socially-average." He meant, I think that we find intelligent authors unable to present any character as heroic who is not just odd or to make any portrayed action expressive of humanity otherwise than by stressing its commonness. This description could serve as a working definition of naturalism. But even so, realism, considered as the alternative and antidote, would have to remain undefined, for it "is not a fixed measure but a variable and comparative achievement." Mention of naturalism and realism would be out of place, because the framework provided by the distinction would be too grand, in a review of almost any contemporary poems. But the poems of Geoffrey Hill are in this, as in many other real ways, exceptional.

Somewhere Is Such a Kingdom makes available in this country the three major collections of Hill's poems that have so far been published in England. These collections are distinct and successful climbs, although there are weak footholds in each of the first two which its successor avoids. Hill's advance, almost from one poem to the next, is so striking and unexpected that it may exhaust anyone who follows it at one sitting through the whole volume. In that sense, the volume does not have its own unity; the parts very much have theirs. Nevertheless I want to make some comparisons between poems not juxtaposed by their author.

Consider first a family of poems about families which includes "The Turtle Dove," "The Troublesome Reign," "Asmodeus, I," "Metamor-

From *The Southern Review* 2, vol. 12 (Spring 1976). Copyright © 1976 by Louisiana State University.

phoses, V," and the third of "Three Baroque Meditations." In six lines of "The Turtle Dove" Hill ascends from the language of a contemporary "voice" like Allen Tate's or Robert Lowell's to a more simple language that echoes the English ballad.

> Love that drained her drained him she'd loved, though each
> For the other's sake forged passion upon speech,
> Bore their close days through sufferance towards night
> Where she at length grasped sleep and he lay quiet
>
> As though needing no questions, now, to guess
> What her secreting heart could not well hide.

The five quatrains of the poem continue the strife of these two languages to a Lawrentian ending. After a period of bleak unlove,

> She went to him, plied there; like a furious dove
> Bore down with visitations of such love
> As his lithe, fathoming heart absorbed and buried.

I presume to associate the more modernist voice here with the pole of the eccentric and the more bardic voice with the pole of the socially-average, following Lukács' suggestion. But it seems to me that Hill takes a step away from the naturalism of this polarity toward a realism, more fully achieved by him elsewhere. The intervening narrative, not yet quoted, boldly uncovers a strong chain of acts. While she

> . . . turned her cheek to the attending world
> Of children and intriguers and the old,
> Conversed freely, exercised, was admired,
> Being strong to dazzle. . . .
>
> He watched her rough grief work
> Under the formed surface of habit.

This plain analysis of compelled lives breathes the air of our time with deliberateness. It is far from the pure idyll of wild possibility which has taken over a part of English poetry since Wallace Stevens (though it would be silly to regard that as his legacy). Describing in "The Troublesome Reign" another difficult match, Hill represents the woman as "feeding a certain green-fuel to his fire./Reluctant heat! This burning of the dead/Could consume her also. . . ." Both poems wear the mode of mere description like stage curtains; behind those curtains they deal with lives threatened with an unspecified despair. "Asmodeus, I" seems to claim a solution to that threat:

Clearly they both stood, lovers without fear,
Might toy with fire brought dangerously to hand
To tame, not exorcise, spirits; though the air
Whistled abstracted menace, could confound
Strength by device, by music reaching the ear,
Lightning conducted forcibly to the ground.

These examples bring out the sense, which runs through Hill's writing, of historical predicaments to be delved or excavated. In the five poems I have grouped together, the toughness and technical assurance of Hill's writing are perhaps more outstanding than any thematic orientation. That they deal with sexual love in a completely uncourtly fashion shows only that they belong to a generation later than Pound's and Eliot's. But that they deal with it instead as an explosive puzzle seems both natural and not easily explained. I propose that it be explained as required for Hill's articulation of a wider historical dialectic. Until recently, the writer as critic of reality was force-fed a world whose unity, no matter what disruptive tensions it contained, was beyond question. Since this situation collapsed, the strongest temptation for the writer-critic has been to equate man's inwardness, which is the root and perhaps the only touchstone of the real world, with either an ineffectual or a morbid playfulness; but in these terms human personality, as a subject to be understood, cannot cohere—something analogous to madness becomes the only human feature accessible to literature. Hill does not yield to this mainstream. His treatment of the lives of the couples in the poems we are considering will not rely upon tricks of illusionism to distract attention away from the medium, and for that reason the lives themselves may seem austere; yet what is really told of them, though reduced to the bone and muscle of description, is not minimal. It promises to expose an underlying form of life that is comprehensive. I am not sure whether it does so. However, in three major sequences, "Funeral Music," "The Songbook of Sebastian Arrurruz," and *Mercian Hymns*, Hill has tried other and finer ways of sifting historical situations for elements out of which to construct a more radical whole.

The first of these sequences is "a commination and an alleluia for the period popularly but inexactly known as the Wars of the Roses." The poems that make it up are blank verse "sonnets" and a comparison between it and Lowell's *History* or parts of that work would shed a favorable light on both, I think. The effect of the whole of "Funeral Music" is not describable in a short space. Here I will only add a note on Hill's flight from naturalism. We do not know who speaks, whether the poet or one of the

victims of the Wars to whom the sequence is dedicated, but the following
statement-of-position puts more forcefully than I can the problematic of
human inwardness mentioned above.

> Though I would scorn the mere instinct of faith,
> Expediency of assent, if I dared,
> What I dare not is a waste history
> Or void rule. Averroes, old heathen,
> If only you had been right, If Intellect
> Itself were absolute law, sufficient grace,
> Our lives could be a myth of captivity
> Which we might enter: an unpeopled region
> Of ever new-fallen snow, a palace blazing
> With perpetual silence as with torches.

What this says about Arabic Platonism is of course less important than its
advocacy, against "a waste history or void rule," of an Aristotelian praxis.
"My mind to me a kingdom is" has serious political meaning in the age
created by the Roses. The very idea of philosophy, as the *Nosce Teipsum*
of Sir John Davies sadly shows, took its English definition from the cramped
and menaced court to whom philosophy was the symbol of retirement from
intrigue and danger. A more noble and important attitude is the engaged
awareness that there could be more to be missed:

> My little son, when you could command marvels
> Without mercy, outstare the wearisome
> Dragon of sleep, I rejoiced above all—
> A stranger well-received in your kingdom.
> On those pristine fields I saw humankind
> As it was named by the Father; fabulous
> Beasts rearing in stillness to be blessed.
> The world's real cries reached there, turbulence
> From remote storms, rumour of solitudes,
> A composed mystery. And so it ends.
> Some parch for what they were; others are made
> Blind to all but one vision, their necessity
> To be reconciled. I believe in my
> Abandonment, since it is what I have.

I think it is no accident that a nativity scene expresses for Hill the "composed mystery" with which "the world's real cries" jar. "Picture of a Nativity" foreshadowed this: the poem has the bearing of Virgil's Eclogue for
Pollio's new son, as if it had been a lucky coincidence that the theme of
an amazing birth is for us a religious and cultural numen:

Sea-preserved, heaped with sea-spoils,
Ribs, keels, coral sores,
Detached faces, ephemeral oils,
Discharged on the world's outer shores,

A dumb child-king
Arrives at his rightful place; rests
Undisturbed, among slack serpents; beasts
With claws flesh-buttered.

But why, except for Hill's Christianity, this should point the way to a resolution of things is not clear to me. How else does what happens "on the world's outer shores" counterbalance "the world's real cries"? But could a religious declaration merit such a place in "Funeral Music"?

"The Songbook of Sebastian Arrurruz" is the work of an apocryphal Spanish poet. The poems invent an English equivalent of the elegant and dispassionate *copla*. The best example is "A Song from Armenia":

Roughly-silvered leaves that are the snow
On Ararat seen through those leaves.
The sun lays down a foliage of shade.

A drinking-fountain pulses its head
Two or three inches from the troughed stone.
An old woman sucks there, gripping the rim.

Why do I have to relive, even now,
Your mouth, and your hand running over me
Deft as a lizard, like a sinew of water?

The relations of the *persona* with his wife are self-consciously investigated in the half-light of "what other men do with other women." The following comparison may at least convey part of the sense of the sequence. This is its last poem:

Scarcely speaking: it becomes as a
Coolness between neighbours. Often
There is this orgy of sleep. I wake
To caress propriety with odd words
And enjoy abstinence in a vocation
Of now-almost-meaningless despair.

There is a shared structure or *parole* in the first of "Four Poems Regarding the Endurance of Poets," a poem dedicated to the memory of Tommaso Campanella, the Masonic priest and poet:

Some days a shadow through
The high window shares my
Prison. I watch a slug
Scale the glinting pit-side
Of its own slime.
. . . we are commanded
To rise, when, in silence,
I would compose my voice.

Solitude, strained interaction with others, and the effect of both on the poet's vocation are hung like the elements of a mobile in each of these two poems. Why such elements hang together is a question which Hill seems to equate with: why should poets see their task as one of criticism anyway? Part of the reply is implicit in the title of "Ovid in the Third Reich" and one line of the poem tells us more explicitly, "Innocence is no earthly weapon." Hill seems to reverse the direction of what is nowadays a common exaggeration: rather than weaken the category of "poet" by denying that label to no one, he identifies human inwardness in general with the regimentation of the classicizing poet.

At least, he seemed to be exploring this identification in *King Log,* his second collection. It is surprisingly absent from *Mercian Hymns,* unless it can be said to be present on the grounds that the new sequence includes autobiographical references. The poems are slightly more restricted than prose poems; they are broken into long prose lines like St.-John Perse's *Anabasis* poems. The sequence often focuses on the Mercian King Offa who "might perhaps most usefully be regarded as the presiding genius of the West Midlands" (Hill's note). But it also focuses, as if by mistake, on Hill as a child:

So much for the elves' wergild, the true governance of England, the
    gaunt warrior-gospel armoured in engraved stone. I wormed my
    way heavenward for ages amid barbaric ivy, scrollwork of fern.
Exile or pilgrim set me once more upon that ground: my rich and
    desolate childhood. Dreamy, smug-faced, sick on outings—I
    who once was taken to be a king of some kind, a prodigy, a
    maimed one.

In one poem he is present as a spectator at a grandmother's (?) funeral: in another he self-righteously "flays" a playmate over a lost toy; in yet another his childhood involvement with history as a subject is given in circumstantial terms. But what ties these poems together is not the mere interest of reminiscence; it is the inner history of the English language or some of that history. In an essay called "Redeeming the Time," Hill has given us

a masterful critical study of the "language-game" that defined the world of
the nineteenth century. His principal thesis or "suggestion" is "that the
epoch was marked by a drastic breaking of tempo and by an equally severe
disturbance of the supposedly normative patterns of speech." It must be
explained that he makes subtle use of the Wittgensteinian notion of a
language-game. One of his comments on the nature of this kind of linguistic
structure recalls Antonio Gramsci's account of the "hegemony" of class
philosophies; for example, he points out that in speaking of language-games
one does not necessarily underrate

> those implicit and explicit tactics whereby a class or faction might contrive
> to project itself as "the world". . . . [That is because] the confines of a
> determined world "give" so as not to give; tropes are predestined to free
> election: the larger determinism allows for the smaller voluntarism.

(It is interesting to compare these last statements with Gramsci's celebrated
rejection of historical determinism.) How does this rarefied framework become concrete in the sequence? Linguistic "tactics" sometimes enter directly
into and are commented on within the same sentence, e.g. "Brooding on
the eightieth letter of *Fors Clavigera,* I speak this in memory of my grandmother, whose childhood and prime womanhood were spent in the nailer's
darg." The book mentioned is of course one of the most overbearing and
preposterous of Ruskin's collections; its praise of simple folk is as oddly
intentioned as its Latin title. As Hill says:

> It is one thing to celebrate the "quick forge," another to cradle a face
> hare-lipped by the searing wire.

Yet it is from Ruskin that Hill gets the word "darg" for a day's work. This
is one of the least complex poems from the standpoint of Hill's interest in
the archeology of language. It would take several paragraphs to comment
even superficially on:

> Where best to stand? Easter sunrays catch the oblique face of Adam
> scrumping through leaves; pale spree of evangelists and, there, a cross
> Christ mumming child Adam out of Hell ('Et exspecto resurrectionem
> mortuorum' dust in the eyes, on clawing wings, and lips)

To suggest that any writing so mannered might struggle with the
fragments of our time and language to construct a realist totality from them
would have shocked the theorist I cited at the outset of this review. But
Lukács cannot have foreseen (with only the Modernists to consider as
concrete evidence) that poetry so self-reflecting could produce, as *Mercian
Hymns* does, so strong a sense of a world with reference to only fragments
of the identities of its inhabitants.

SEAMUS HEANEY

An English Mason

Stone and rock figure prominently in
the world of Geoffrey Hill's poetry . . . but Hill's imagination is not content
to grant the mineral world the absolute sway that Hughes allows it. He is
not the suppliant chanting to the megalith, but rather the mason dressing
it. Hill also beats the bounds of an England facing into the Celtic mysteries
of Wales and out towards the military and ecclesiastical splendours of Europe. His most recent book names his territory Mercia, and masks his
imagination under the figure of King Offa, builder of Offa's dyke between
England and Wales, builder as well as beater of the boundaries. Hill's
celebration of Mercia has a double-focus: one a child's-eye view, close to
the common earth, the hoard of history, and the other the historian's and
scholar's eye, inquisitive of meaning, bringing time past to bear on time
present and vice versa. But the writing itself is by no means abstract and
philosophical. Hill addresses the language, as I say, like a mason addressing
a block, not unlike his own mason in Hymn XXIV:

> Itinerant through numerous domains, of his lord's
>   retinue, to Compostela. Then home for a lifetime
>   amid West Mercia this master-mason as I envisage
>   him, intent to pester upon tympanum and chancel-
>   arch his moody testament, confusing warrior with
>   lion, dragon-coils, tendrils of the stony vine.

> Where best to stand? Easter sunrays catch the ob-
>   lique face of Adam scrumping through leaves; pale
>   spree of evangelists and, there, a cross Christ
>   mumming child Adam out of Hell

From *Critical Inquiry* 3, vol. 3 (Spring 1977). Copyright © 1977 by The University of
Chicago Press.

('Et exspecto resurrectionem mortuorum' dust in the
eyes, on clawing wings, and lips)

Not only must English be kept up here, with its "spree" and "scrumping" and "mumming," but Latin and learning must be kept up too. The mannered rhetoric of these pieces is a kind of verbal architecture, a grave and sturdy English Romanesque. The native undergrowth, both vegetative and verbal, that barbaric scrollwork of fern and ivy, is set against the tympanum and chancel-arch, against the weighty elegance of imperial Latin. The overall pattern of his language is an extension and a deliberate exploitation of the lingustic effect in Shakespeare's famous lines, "It would the multitudinous seas incarnadine,/Making the green one red," where the polysyllabic flourish of "multitudinous" and "incarnadine" is both set off and undercut by the monosyllabic plainness of "making the green one red," where the Latinate and the local also go hand in glove. There is in Hill something of Stephen Dedalus's hyperconsciousness of words as physical sensations, as sounds to be plumbed, as weights on the tongue. Words in his poetry fall slowly and singly, like molten solder, and accumulate to a dull glowing nub. I imagine Hill as indulging in a morose linguistic delectation, dwelling on the potential of each word with much the same slow relish as Leopold Bloom dwells on the thought of his kidney. And in *Mercian Hymns,* in fact, Hill's procedure resembles Joyce's not only in this linguistic deliberation and self-consciousness. For all his references to the "precedent provided by the Latin prose-hymns or canticles of the early Christian Church," what these hymns celebrate is the "ineluctable modality of the audible," as well as the visible, and the form that celebration takes reminds one of the Joycean epiphany, which is a prose poem in effect. But not only in the form of the individual pieces, but in the overall structuring of the pieces, he follows the Joycean precedent set in *Ulysses* of confounding modern autobiographical material with literary and historic matter drawn from the past. Offa's story makes contemporary landscape and experience live in the rich shadows of a tradition.

To go back to Hymn XXIV, the occasion, the engendering moment, seems to involve the contemplation of a carved pediment—a tympanum is the cubical head of a pediment—which exhibits a set of scenes: one of Eden, one of some kind of harrowing of hell; and the scenes are supervised by images of the evangelists. And this cryptic, compressed mode of presentation in which a few figures on stone can call upon the whole body of Christian doctrines and mythology resembles the compression of the piece itself. The carving reminds him of the carver, a master mason—and the relevant note reads: "for the association of Compostela with West Midlands sculpture of the twelfth century I am indebted to G. Zarnecki, *Later English Romanesque Sculpture,* London (1953)." This mason is "itinerant"—a word used in its precise Latin sense, yet when applied to a traveling craftsman, that pristine sense seems to foreshadow its present narrowed meaning of tinker, a travelling tinsmith, a white-smith. In the first phrases the Latinate predominates, for this is a ritual progress, an itinerary "through numerous domains, of his Lord's retinue," to Compostela. Even the proper name flaps out its music like some banner there. But when he gets home, he is momentarily cut down from his grand tour importance to his homely size, in the simple "Then home for a lifetime amid West Mercia"; but now the poet/observer of the carving has caught something of the sense of occasion and borrowed something of the mason's excitement. yet he does not "see in the mind's eye," like Hamlet, but "envisages" him, the verb being properly liturgical, "intent to pester upon tympanum and chancel-arch his moody testament, confusing warrior with lion, dragon-coils . . ." Tympanum, of course, is also a drum, and the verb "pester" manages a rich synaesthetic effect; the stone is made to cackle like a kettle drum as the chisel hits it. But "pester" is more interesting still. Its primary meaning, from the original Latin root, *pastorium,* means to hobble a horse, and it was used in 1685 to mean "crowding persons in or into." So the mason hobbles and herds and crowds in warrior and lion, dragon coils, tendrils of the stony vine; and this interlacing and entanglement of motifs is also the method of the poem.

In fact, we can see the method more clearly if we put the poem in its proper context, which is in the middle of a group of three entitled *Opus Anglicanum.* Once again the note is helpful:

> '*Opus Anglicanum*': the term is properly applicable to English embroidery of the period AD 1250–1350, though the craft was already famous some centuries earlier. . . . I have, with considerable impropriety, extended the term to apply to English Romanesque sculpture and to utilitarian metal-work of the nineteenth century.

The entanglement, the interlacing, is now that of embroidery, and this first poem, I suggest, brings together womanly figures from Hill's childhood memory with the ghostly procession of needleworkers from the medieval castles and convents:

XXIII

In tapestries, in dreams, they gathered, as it was en-
acted, the return, the re-entry of transcendence
into this sublunary world. *Opus Anglicanum,* their

> stringent mystery riddled by needles: the silver
> veining, the gold leaf, voluted grape-vine, master-
> works of treacherous thread.

> They trudged out of the dark, scraping their boots
> free from lime-splodges and phlegm. They munched
> cold bacon. The lamps grew plump with oily re-
> liable light.

Again, you'll notice the liturgical and Latinate of the first paragraph abraded and rebutted by the literal and local weight of "scraping their boots free from lime-splodges and phlegm"—the boots being, I take it, the boots of labourers involved in the never-ending *Opus Anglicanum*, from agricultural origins to industrial developments. And in order just to clinch the thing, I'll read the third piece, where the "utilitarian iron work" in which his grandmother was involved is contemplated in a perspective that includes medieval embroidress and mason, and a certain "transcendence" enters the making of wire nails:

XXV

> Brooding on the eightieth letter of *Fors Clavigera*,
> I speak this in memory of my grandmother, whose
> childhood and prime womanhood were spent in the
> nailer's darg.

> The nailshop stood back of the cottage, by the fold.
> It reeked stale mineral sweat. Sparks had furred
> its low roof. In dawn-light the troughed water
> floated a damson-bloom of dust—

> not to be shaken by posthumous clamour. It is one
> thing to celebrate the 'quick forge', another
> to cradle a face hare-lipped by the searing wire.

> Brooding on the eightieth letter of *Fors Clavigera*,
> I speak this in memory of my grandmother, whose
> childhood and prime womanhood were spent in the
> nailer's drag.

Ruskin's eightieth letter reflects eloquently and plangently on the injustice of the master and servant situation, on the exploitation of labour, on the demeaning work in a nail forge. The Mayor of Birmingham took him to a house where two women were at work, labouring, as he says, with ancient Vulcanian skill:

> So wrought they,—the English matron and maid;—so it was their darg
> to labour from morning to evening—seven to seven—by the furnace side—
> the winds of summer fanning the blast of it.

He goes on to compute that the woman and the husband earned altogether £55 a year with which to feed and clothe themselves and their six children, to reproach the luxury of the mill-owning class, and to compare the waves of industrialists contemplating Burne Jones's picture of Venus's mirror, "with these, their sisters, who had only, for Venus's mirror, a heap of ashes; compassed about with no forget-me-nots, but with all the forget-fulness in the world."

It seems to me here that Hill is celebrating his own indomitable Englishry, casting his mind on other days, singing a clan beaten into the clay and ashes, and linking their patience, their sustaining energy, with the glory of England. The "quick forge," after all, may be what its origin in Shakespeare's *Henry V* declares it to be, "the quick forge and working house of thought," but it is surely also the "random grim forge" of Felix Randall, the farrier. The image shuttles between various points and weaves a new *opus anglicanum* in this intended and allusive poem. And the hard driving point of the shuttle, of course, is forged with *darg*, that chip off the Anglo-Saxon block, meaning "a day's work, or the task of a day."

The *Mercian Hymns* show Hill in full command of his voice. Much as the stiff and corbelled rhetoric of earlier work like *Funeral Music* and "Requiem for the Plantagenet Kings" stands up and will stand up, it is only when this rhetoric becomes a press tightening on and squeezing out of the language the vigour of common speech, the essential Anglo-Saxon juices, it is only then that the poetry attains this final refreshed and refreshing quality: then he has, in the words of another piece, accrued a "golden and stinking blaze."

CHRISTOPHER RICKS

"*The Tongue's Atrocities*"

Aprincipled distrust of the imagi-
nation is nothing new. One triumph of the imagination is that it can be
aware of the perils of the imagination, the aggrandisements, covert in-
dulgences, and specious claims which it may incite. Great art is often about
the limits of what we should hope for even from the greatest of art, and
among the many things which the imagination can realize on our behalf,
one such is the limits of the sympathetic imagination.

A poem by Geoffrey Hill speaks of 'The tongue's atrocities' ('History
as Poetry'), compacting or colluding the atrocities of which the tongue
must speak, with the atrocities which—unless it is graced with unusually
creative vigilance—it is all too likely to commit when it speaks of atrocities.
For atrocity may get flattened down into the casually 'atrocious', or it may
get fattened up into that debased form of imagination which is prurience.
So the general burden of the imagination's self-scrutiny presses particularly
upon all such art as contemplates (in both senses) atrocities.

In his literary criticism, Geoffrey Hill has worried at this, as when
he praised the poetry with which Ben Jonson both fleshes and cauterizes
the atrocities of imperial Rome: 'Jonson's qualifications worry the verse into
dogs-teeth of virtuous self-mistrust'; and again when Hill praised the 'terrible
beauty' of Yeats's 'Easter 1916': 'the tune of a mind distrustful yet envious,
mistrusting the abstraction, mistrusting its own mistrust'. This subject of
much of Hill's criticism is the impulse of much of his poetry. 'Annunciations: I' is about art as connoisseurship (for its creators as much as for its
audiences or critics—Hill never makes a complacent distinction between
the likes of him and the likes of us). 'The Humanist' and 'The Imaginative

Life' are both impelled by virtuous self-mistrust; 'The Martyrdom of Saint Sebastian' bends its attention upon the glazing of the martyr's pains.

The act of imagining, and of inscribing in words, can so easily claim 'too much or too little'. The prose-poem which uses those words, 'Offa's Sword' (*Mercian Hymns*), ponders the great gift brought to Offa: 'The Frankish gift, two-edged, regaled with slaughter'. Regaled, with its regalia (and *regalo* means a gift); but 'regaled with slaughter' opens up a grim fissure—the poem uses the word 'fissured'—between the barbaric opulence and the jaded prurience: regaled with good stories, with Christmas fare (the poem speaks of 'Christ's mass'), and with deliciously domesticated slaughter. 'Two-edged'.

But let me quote Hill's most explicit imagining of prurience as imagination's dark double, 'Offa's Journey to Rome':

> At Pavia, a visitation of some sorrow. Boethius'
> dungeon. He shut his eyes, gave rise to a tower
> out of the earth. He willed the instruments of
> violence to break upon meditation. Iron buckles
> gagged; flesh leaked rennet over them; the men
> stooped, disentangled the body.

> He wiped his lips and hands. He strolled back to the
> car, with discreet souvenirs for consolation and
> philosophy. He set in motion the furtherance of
> his journey. To watch the Tiber foaming out
> much blood.

See how 'gave rise to' is redeemed from its heartless officialese; and how the very instruments of imprisonment ought to have vomited (to have gagged in gagging him); and how the body becomes that of an unweaned calf, its rennet curdling; and how the poem itself honourably fears the feasting prurience of all such imaginings: 'He wiped his lips and hands'. Can we remember such things without reducing them to discreet souvenirs? Is even God above such diseased imaginings? God, 'voyeur of sacrifice'. But it is characteristic of Hill to have deitalicised the word 'voyeur' when he reprinted that poem after its first publication ('Locust Songs')—who are the English to imply that voyeurism is foreign to them? A comment by Hill on 'Annunciations: II' might stand as an epigraph to all such poems of his: 'But I want the poem to have this dubious end; because I feel dubious; and the whole business is dubious'.

Yet upon this ancient dubiety, which is not a failure of nerve but an acknowledgement of what a success of nerve might be, there has been urged in the last forty years a unique and hideous modern intensification.

The Nazi extermination-camps are a horror which has been felt to dwarf all art and to paralyse all utterance. There would be something suspect about anybody who felt nothing of the impulse which voiced itself in George Steiner as 'The world of Auschwitz lies outside speech as it lies outside reason'. But then this very impulse can uglily become a routine, a mannerism, or a cliché. There is something oppressively to-be-expected about beginning a book on *The Holocaust and the Literary Imagination* (1975) with a chapter entitled 'In the Beginning Was the Silence', with its epigraph from Beckett: 'Speech is a desecration of silence', and with the first sentence invoking Adorno's cry that to write poetry after Auschwitz is barbaric. A poet may feel that not only is Auschwitz unspeakable but that this fear itself has become unsayable, so much said as scarcely to be accessible to feeling. There press upon all these grim doubts and realities both a harsh unignorability and a smoothly righteous triteness.

Geoffrey Hill was born in 1932. He is in my judgment the best of those English poets who entered into adult consciousness in the post-war, not the pre-war or the war-time, world. Poets just older than Hill—Philip Larkin, say—were in possession of a conscious experienced public conscious when the news and then the newsreels of Belsen and Auschwitz disclosed the atrocities. A poet of exactly Hill's age did not yet possess any such experienced conscience; Hill was thirteen in 1945, and he belongs to the generation whose awakening to the atrocity of adult life was an awakening to this unparalleled atrocity. It is true that no Englishman had ever before known anything like those newsreels, those photographs, those histories; but Englishmen older than Hill did not have this atrocity as their first introduction to atrocity. Hill wrote his first poems in the late 1940's; mercifully, there is every reason to believe that the poems were not bent upon the Nazi holocaust. But since then, he has written the deepest and truest poems on that holocaust: 'September Song', and 'Ovid in the Third Reich', as well as a few other poems on this atrocity which are honourable, fierce and grave: 'Two Formal Elegies', 'Domaine Public', and section IV in 'Of Commerce and Society':

> Statesmen have known visions. And, not alone,
> Artistic men prod dead men from their stone:
> Some of us have heard the dead speak:
> The dead are my obsession this week
>
> But may be lifted away. In summer
> Thunder may strike, or, as a tremor
> Of remote adjustment, pass on the far side
> From us: however deified and defied

> By those it does strike. Many have died. Auschwitz,
> Its furnace chambers and lime pits
> Half-erased, is half-dead; a fable
> Unbelievable in fatted marble.
>
> There is, at times, some need to demonstrate
> Jehovah's touchy methods, that create
> The connoisseur of blood, the smitten man.
> At times it seems not common to explain.

The dignified force of Hill's poetry on such atrocity is a matter of his grasping that the atrocity both is and is not unique, and that it presents to the imagination a challenge which likewise both is and is not unique. Hill does not permit the Jews' sufferings to be separated from or aloof from the other hideous sufferings which fill the air of the past and the present. It is characteristic of him that he should not countenance the well-meant but misguided turn which would monopolize the word 'holocaust' for the sufferings of the Jews. He does not withhold the word from the Jews (though not in the dangerous form 'the Holocaust'), and this not least because he feels dismay at the unjustly retributive irony of the word's etymology and its religious allegiance: 'A sacrifice wholly consumed by fire; a whole burnt offering'. But he would support neither monopoly nor pedantry, and he says of the Battle of Towton (Palm Sunday, 1461): 'In the accounts of the contemporary chroniclers it was a holocaust'.

This poem, 'Statesmen have known visions . . .', is a poem which knows what it is up against. Its pained rhythms resist both a facile self-exculpation and a facile self-inculpation. 'The dead are my obsession this week': the rhythm is at once strong and strained, and it protects the groundedly sardonic against the ingratiatingly self-deprecating. It is doubly styptic. As is the turn which first grimly shrivels 'deified' down into 'defied' and then shrivels them both down to 'died'. 'Many have died'. 'Deified' into 'defied' is a genuine but precarious movement of the imagination; so the subsequent pared-down 'died' rightly does not disown it, but does place and weigh it. Against that laconic shrivelling root-simplicity is set the grossly burgeoning unimaginability of Auschwitz, with the very sounds moving from delicacy ('a fable') into the fattened slabs of monumental evil:

> a fable
> Unbelievable in fatted marble.

For '*fatted marble*' is a distending of the word 'fable' into a sleek stoniness; and 'fatted' is the ancient sacrifice. To 'pass on the far side' may at the time be well-judged but may also later be harshly judged. The poem is forced to ask, at least, about the relation between the Jews and their God:

> There is, at times, some need to demonstrate
> Jehovah's touchy methods, that create
> The connoisseur of blood, the smitten man.
> At times it seems not common to explain.

For 'the smitten man' is a thrust at one of those moments when the God of the Jews moves in an appallingly mysterious way:

> And a certain man of the sons of the prophets said unto his neighbour in the word of the Lord, Smite me, I pray thee. And the man refused to smite him. Then said he unto him, Because thou hast not obeyed the voice of the Lord, behold, as soon as thou art departed from me, a lion shall slay thee. And as soon as he was departed from him, a lion found him, and slew him. Then he found another man, and said, Smite me, I pray thee. And the man smote him, so that in smiting he wounded him.
>
> (*I Kings,* xx 37)

'At times it seems not common to explain'. Which is not to say that the poem asks us to accept the cliché, the common explanation. For the 'unbelievable' is also the unexplainable, and the world of Hill's poem is completely different from the world of George Steiner's prose with its explanation of why all this befell the Jews: 'the blackmail of perfection' which the Jews three times visited upon Western life: the intolerable idealisms of, first, monotheism; then Christian adjuration; then messianic socialism. 'When it turned on the Jew, Christianity and European civilization turned on the incarnation—albeit an incarnation often wayward and unaware—of its own best hopes'.

> Statesmen have known visions. And, not alone,
> Artistic men prod dead men from their stone.

Hill has pronounced

TWO FORMAL ELEGIES
For the Jews in Europe

I

> Knowing the dead, and how some are disposed:
> Subdued under rubble, water, in sand graves,
> In clenched cinders not yielding their abused
> Bodies and bonds to those whom war's chance saves
> Without the law: we grasp, roughly, the song.
> Arrogant acceptance from which song derives
> Is bedded with their blood, makes flourish young
> Roots in ashes. The wilderness revives,

Deceives with sweetness harshness. Still beneath
Live skin stone breathes, about which fires but play,
Fierce heart that is the iced brain's to command
To judgment—(studied reflex, contained breath)—
Their best of worlds since, on the ordained day,
This world went spinning from Jehovah's hand.

II

For all that must be gone through, their long death
Documented and safe, we have enough
Witnesses (our world being witness-proof).
The sea flickers, roars, in its wide hearth.
Here, yearly, the pushing midlanders stand
To warm themselves; men, brawny with life,
Women who expect life. They relieve
Their thickening bodies, settle on scraped sand.

Is it good to remind them, on a brief screen,
Of what they have witnessed and not seen?
(Deaths of the city that persistently dies . . . ?)
To put up stones ensures some sacrifice.
Sufficient men confer, carry their weight.
(At whose door does the sacrifice stand or start?)

The first poem, which begins with the dangerous word 'Knowing', knows that our comprehension of it will have to be a matter of grasping it, with some of the urgent haste of such seizing. Like its creator, 'we grasp, roughly, the song'. *Roughly* as untenderly (how else can we resist the solicitations of a false tenderness—'Knowing the dead'? But, like Hill, we never did know them as people known to us; and a sense of threat swells within that other dark meaning of 'knowing the dead. . . .'—and what they are capable of). But *roughly*, too, as approximately (to hope for more than an honourable approximation in such a case would be dishonourable hubris).

There is an angry vibration in this response to the outraged dead. Life, bristling against injustice, quivers in the restive play upon *disposed*: 'Knowing the dead, and how some are disposed'—a disposition of mind, or the disposal of a body? Likewise in *subdued*: 'Subdued under rubble'—a crushed body, or a quietly stoical mind? The quivering of life is there again in the bitter archaism of 'war's chance': 'those whom war's chance saves'. For where in the world of technologized extermination is there even a memory of what was once true and poignant: 'The chance of war / Is equal and the slayer oft is slain' (*The Iliad*)? There is the old sense of outrage felt yet once more, in the mingled gratitude to and warning to Voltaire: 'Their best of worlds'. There is the simultaneous delight and fear in 'This world went spinning from Jehovah's hand': spinning effortlessly into its ordained arc, or spinning away for ever from his hand?

In the second poem, there is the same glowering intensity alive to the terrible questions which ask what good it can do even to think on these things, truly knowing that it may well do ill. 'For all that must be gone through': for all which, or—with the known acknowledged *that* as either shouldered or shrugged off—'For all that must be gone through'. Gone through, as endured, or as wearisomely enumerated? How hostile the relation is between 'witness' and 'proof', held apart and together by their hyphen: 'witness-proof', and then between 'witness-proof' and fireproof or foolproof. What are we proofed in, armoured in, that we think we can witness, let alone bear witness to, such happenings? The 'midlanders', after all, are English tourists as well as Mediterranean natives. With the last line of the second poem, there ignites the fierceness which was smouldering in the firm poem. For 'Without the law' had not forgotten Kipling's 'Recessional':

> Such boastings as the Gentiles use,
>   Or lesser breeds without the Law—
> Lord God of Hosts, be with us yet,
> Lest we forget—lest we forget!

No tremor passes through Kipling's line: 'Still stands Thine ancient sacrifice'. Hill's final line has the tremor of genuine interrogation: '(At whose door does the sacrifice stand or start?)' 'The guilt of blood is at your door', wrote Tennyson. And *start* is a last twist: jump in shock (as against the stolid *stand*), or learn to begin? Hill, who says in another poem about the dead that 'Some, finally, learn to begin' ('The Distant Fury of Battle'), ends this poem with a sudden 'start'; he has brought us to the point at which we may indeed start.

These are poems which carry their weight, and they are substantially resistant, so there remain many serious questions as to how to construe and what to make of them. But I wish to move to a consideration which then bears on others of Hill's poems, a consideration which becomes manifest in the revisions which Hill made to this poem after its first publication. As originally published, it had within brackets the dedication '(For the Jews of Europe)', and the second poem then ended with an extraordinary tour-de-force: of the last four lines, not only the first and the last were each within brackets, but so too were the second and the third. The poem ended with four successive lines each within brackets. Hill was right to think that his is a poetic gift which must be profoundly and variously alive to what simple brackets can do. He had been wrong to think that he could command to favourable judgment a concatenation of four lines, each bracketed, without his poem's indurating itself into mannerism and self-attention, a sequence of self-containednesses such as then seals the poem into self-congratulation. By removing the brackets from both the antepenultimate and the penultimate lines, he not only removed the oppression of paralysing self-consciousness, but also tautened the arc of the poem. For, unlike the first poem, the second has at last gravitated to couplets; against which there is now played a beautiful and complementary chiasmus, a/b/b/a, in the sombre punctuation alone. Of the last four lines, the first and second, and then the third and fourth, rhyme together, but it is the second and third, and then the first and fourth, which punctuate together. The tensions of the last four lines now dispose themselves differently; less disruptedly, less fracturedly, and more finally, since chiasmus comprises an arc.

Brackets are a way of containing things and feelings, in both of the senses of containing: including and restraining. It is then a true sense of the metaphorical power even of ordinary punctuation which led Hill to have, as the only parenthesis within the first poem, the words '—(studied reflex, contained breath)—'. The parenthesis holds the breadth of the dead; we hold our breath, and contain ourselves, even as the speaking poet does, with his syntax suspended and his rhythm tensed (a steadying of the voice is necessary in 'contained breath', with its minute resistance to the iambic movement), so that, at once trained and spontaneous—'(studied reflex, contained breath)'—, the lines may 'command to judgment . . . Their best of worlds'.

There is a different kind of metaphorical life in the parenthesis in the second poem: '(our world being witness-proof)'. For here the brackets suggest the corrupt separateness of which contained breath is the pure counterpart; the brackets now act as a kind of proof or armour against all penetrative imagination, with *our world* fortified in blasé imperviousness by its brackets, unlike their open hope, 'Their best of worlds', 'this world'. The two other bracketings (two from what, as I have said, had been four) embody a move from one kind of musing, a brooding upon a paradox such as may be religious or religiose, musing into the truth-gathering or the wool-gathering of three dots: '(Deaths of the city that persistently dies . . . ?)'— a move from this kind of musing into something much sharper in sound and sense, a 'perplexed persistence', a baffled indictment: '(At whose door does the sacrifice stand or start?) Yet the end is at once curt and muted— muted by the inevitably receding or *recessional* quality of brackets as we read them.

But 'read them' is equivocal. Eyes and ears? Although our inner ear may divine a tone from such brackets, may sense a lowering of the timbre or pitch or tone or note or simply loudness, one of the important things about brackets is that they belong with those signs of punctuation which the voice cannot sufficiently utter. Hill's poetry makes weighty and delicate use of this very fact. Hugh Kenner has pointed out that you cannot say a footnote or an asterisk; I disagree with him about parentheses.

> The footnote's relation to the passage from which it depends is established wholly by visual and typographic means, and will typically defeat all efforts of the speaking voice to clarify it without visual aid. Parentheses, like commas, tell the voice what to do: an asterisk tells the voice that it can do nothing. You cannot read a passage of prose aloud, interpolating the footnotes, and make the subordination of the footnotes clear, and keep the whole sounding natural. The language has forsaken a vocal milieu, and a context of oral communication between persons, and commenced to take advantage of the expressive possibilities of technological space.

This is entirely true of the footnote and the asterisk; perhaps the auditory imagination, when the eye reads such punctuation, hears something, calls up some tone to itself for what it is apprehending, but this auditory imagination is essentially private. You could not, in the manner of French dictation at school, read aloud such punctuation and elicit accurate transcriptions from your hearers, any more than you could of T. S. Eliot's spacing-punctuation in *The Waste Land*. The eye can here allow to enter its consciousness what the tongue cannot then utter.

But Kenner is wrong to set up the contrast: 'Parentheses, like commas, tell the voice what to do: an asterisk tells the voice that it can do nothing'. For though a parenthesis is a syntactical unit, and of course the voice can make such a thing clear, a parenthesis is a syntactical unit which may be qualified by very different punctuations. *Parenthesis:* 'An explanatory or qualifying word, clause, or sentence inserted into a passage with which it has not necessarily any grammatical connexion, and from which it is usually marked off by round or square brackets, dashes, or commas' *(OED)*. We use the word parenthesis both for the unit and for one of the many ways of indicating it, and the voice is not able to make adequately clear (adequate in both delicacy and clarity) whether the parenthesis is bracketed off, comma'd off, or dashed off. (Even apart from the fact that the voice cannot utter a square as against a round bracket.) For although it may be true that such punctuation as is markedly durational may be uttered (a full stop is likely, though only likely, to mean a longer pause than a comma), the thing about brackets is that they are not essentially an indicator of duration. They indicate a relationship which may or may not have a durational dimension, and they speak to the eye and not to the ear. A poet who has a strong sense both of all that the voice can do and of all that it cannot, a poet who knows that the timing within a poem both is and is not a matter of tempo, will be a poet who seizes upon the particular power of the bracket to incarnate something which commands a sense of the difference between what can be printedly read and what can be said.

It is Hill's 'September Song' which most fully realizes, in both senses, how much a simple point of punctuation may weigh.

SEPTEMBER SONG
born 19.6.32—deported 24.9.42

> Undesirable you may have been, untouchable
> you were not. Not forgotten
> or passed over at the proper time.
>
> As estimated, you died. Things marched,
> sufficient, to that end.
> Just so much Zyklon and leather, patented
> terror, so many routine cries.
>
> (I have made
> an elegy for myself it
> is true)
>
> September fattens on vines. Roses
> flake from the wall. The smoke
> of harmless fires drifts to my eyes.
>
> This is plenty. This is more than enough.

It is a poem which has elicited from Jon Silkin a sustained critical meditation, which I shall quote in its entirety:

> A concentration camp victim. Even the 'play' in the subtitle 'born 19.6.32—deported 24.9.42' where the natural event of the birth is placed, simply, beside the human and murderous 'deported' as if the latter were of the same order and inevitability for the victim; which, in some senses, it was—even here, the zeugmatic wit is fully employed. The irony of conjuncted meanings between 'undesirable' (touching on both sexual desire and racism) and 'untouchable', which exploits a similar ambiguity but reverses the emphases, is unusually dense *and* simple. The confrontation is direct and unavoidable, and this directness is brought to bear on the reader not only by the vocabulary, but by the balancing directness of the syntax. This stanza contains one of Hill's dangerous words—dangerous because of its too-frequent use, and because these words sometimes unleash (though not here) a too evident irony:

> Not forgotten
> or passed over at the proper time.

'Proper' brings together the idea of bureaucratically correct 'as calculated' by the logistics of the 'final solution' and the particular camp's timetable; it also contrasts the idea of the mathematically 'correct' with the morally intolerable. It touches, too, on the distinction between what is morally right, and what is conventionally acceptable, and incidentally brings to bear on the whole the way in which the conventionally acceptable is often used to cloak the morally unacceptable. One of Hill's grim jokes, deployed in such a way that the laughter is precisely proportionate to the needs of ironic exposure. It is when the irony is in excess of the situation that the wit becomes mannered. But here it does not. So the poem continues, remorselessly.

> As estimated, you died. Things marched,
> sufficient, to that end.

One feels the little quibbling movement in

> As estimated, you died

as, without wishing to verbalise it, Hill points to the disturbing contrast between the well-functioning time-table and what it achieved. 'Things marched' has the tread of pompous authority, immediately, in the next line, qualified by the painfully accurate recognition that just so much energy was needed, and released, for the extermination. 'Sufficient' implies economy, but it also implies a conscious qualification of the heavy, pompous tread of authority. The quiet function of unpretentious machinery fulfilled its programme, perhaps *more* lethally. One also notices here how the lineation gauges, exactly, the flow and retraction of meaning and impulse, and how this exact rhythmical flow is so much a part of the sensuous delivery of response and evaluation. It is speech articulated, but the lineation provides, via the convention of verse line-ending, a formal control of rhythm, and of sense emphasis, by locking with, or breaking, the syntactical flow. Thus in the third stanza the syntax is broken by the lineation exactly at those parts at which the confession, as it were, of the poem's (partial) source is most painful:

> (I have made
> an elegy for myself it
> is true)

The slightly awkward break after 'it' not only forces the reading speed down to a word-by-word pace, in itself an approximation to the pain of the confession, but emphasises the whole idea. By placing emphasis on the unspecifying pronoun, Hill is able to say two things: that the elegy was made for himself (at least, in part) since in mourning another one is also commiserating with one's own condition.

> When we chant
> 'Ora, ora pro nobis' it is not
> Seraphs who descend to pity but ourselves.
> ('Funeral Music')

But 'it' may also refer to the whole event; I have made an elegy for myself, as we all do, but I have also made an elegy on a 'true' event. True imaginatively, true in detailed fact; both for someone other than myself. Thus he is able to point to the difficulty of the poet, who wishes, for a variety of reasons, to approach the monstrousness of such events, but has compunction about doing so. He tactfully touches for instance on the overweening ambition of the poet who hitches his talent to this powerful subject, thereby giving his work an impetus it *may* not be fully entitled to, since, only the victim, herself, would be entitled to derive this kind of 'benefit'. But he also modestly pleads, I think, with 'it / is true' that whatever the reasons for his writing such an elegy, a proper regard for the victim, a true and unambitious feeling, was present and used.

Silkin's sense of the poem is scrupulous and touching. The poem is indeed 'dense *and* simple'; so I should add that, for instance, the awful weight upon

> Not forgotten
> or passed over at the proper time

is instinct not only with the bitter reversal of the Passover (with its further flickering reminder that innocent Egyptians and not just guilty ones were smitten with the loss of their first-born), but also with the petty grievance of promotion denied: 'passed over'. Similar vibrations stir in the dehumanizing militaristic bureaucracy of 'Things marched', and in the tiny dubiety of 'Just so much . . .', where 'Just' is both the casually murderous 'Merely' and the meticulously murderous 'Precisely'. 'Zyklon' is then, in every sense, a word from—a wafting of poison gas from—a completely different world from that of everything else in the poem, unutterably alien and not just foreign; ugly; imperious (Hill had originally given it only a lower-case z, which too much lowered its hateful rank)—a word (is it a *word*, even?) which did not have this 'patented' sense until our time, scarcely belongs in the English language, and which is now for ever doomed to the detestation of one immediate association. There it is, capitalized, in this poem which has no name for the dead child. Then there is the sickening glissade from *leather* to *patented*, and the awful possibility of fatigued exasperation in 'so many routine cries'. Routine cries, to the camp's officials; can a poem raise itself above a routine cry?

The poem moves through from two groupings (they can't be called stanzas) which are 'you', through two which are 'I' and 'my', to a bleak

curt shaping (one line only) which is neither 'you' nor 'I'. 'This is plenty.
This is more than enough'. This? This, as the smiling month of September,
a mockery of that September in 1942, which itself had mocked the month
of the Jewish New Year and of the Day of Atonement. The anger at the
month is unjust, casting-about for a scapegoat: 'September fattens on
vines'—again the basking fatness, being fattened for the kill, a fertilising
richness. But then there is the other 'This'—This, as the attempt to speak
of it (it, the further 'This,' the happening itself). Bitter at the ineffectuality
of even its own best efforts, and so dismissing them curtly and yet with
the reluctance of repetition: 'This is plenty. This is more than enough'.
Plenty, as gratitude to nature's foison, but also as brusque slang; 'more than
enough', as needing to end in something more English, an unillusioned
understatement. The last line pounces, and yet its cadence doesn't fall into
the trap which waits for the separate finality of that old reassurance, the
clinching iambic pentameter. Partly this is a matter of the delicacy which
which it both is and is not preceded by an iambic pentameter: 'The smoke
/ of harmless fires drifts to my eyes'. That is not one line, but one and a
half; the cadence drifts across, and then what had been drifting suddenly
clenches itself. Yet not into anything easily clinching, since the one line
is both one and two in its structure: 'This is plenty. This is more than
enough'. Behind the poet's pinched self-scrutiny, having to bite back, we
should poignantly hear the age-old open-hearted fierce gratitude with which
the Jews thank their God at Passover:

> If he had brought us forth out of Egypt but had not executed
> judgments upon the Egyptians, it would have been enough.
> If he had executed judgments upon the Egyptians, but had not
> executed judgments upon their gods, it would have been enough.
> If he had executed judgments upon their gods, but had not slain
> their first-born, it would have been enough.
> If he had slain their first-born, but had not bestowed their wealth
> on us, it would have been enough.
> If he had bestowed their wealth on us, but had not divided the sea
> for us, it would have been enough . . .

Jon Silkin feels, and helps us feel, the central gravity of the three
lines

> (I have made
> an elegy for myself it
> is true)

But I believe that it is crucial to them that they are in brackets. For it is
this, and not their tone or syntax alone, which gives them that unique

feeling of being at once a crux and an aside, at once an inescapable hon-ourable admission and something which the poem may then honourably pass over. It is the brackets which embody the essential discrimination between the right and the wrong kind of detachment. Hopkins may tell his autumnal griever that she is grieving not for Goldengrove but for herself: 'It is Margaret you mourn for'. Hill acknowledges that he mourns for himself, but he refuses to make the total concession which would evacuate the whole matter; he does not say that he has made an elegy only for himself; and 'it is true'—which is unsayably punctuated so that only the eye can sense its utterance—is not only the concession, and not only an insistence that the deportation indeed happened, but also a quietly confident insistence that the elegy itself is true.

For its truth is partly that it embodies the truth that what happened was unspeakable, and at the heart of the poem is this moment of something that is perfectly lucid but unspeakable, unsayable. A man may write of it, and that is not nothing, but he cannot *speak* of it, any more than you can speak those brackets. If you know that there are brackets there, you can strain to hear them; and the eye may be deeply moved by the way in which the brackets lower the words within them down into silent depths. But they intimate an irreducible recalcitrance, of the kind which any true poem on such atrocities ought to intimate. 'The tongue's atrocities': but these bracketed words protect themselves against the tongue and its arts.

WILLIAM S. MILNE

'Creative Tact': "King Log"

Eight of the poems in Hill's second book of poetry, *King Log* (André Deutsch, 1968) first appeared in his Northern House Poets pamphlet, *Preghiere* (School of English, University of Leeds, 1964). Nine poems from *King Log* had been previously printed in *Penguin Modern Poets* 8 (1966)—the eight poems from *Preghiere* ('Men are a mockery of angels'; 'Domaine public'; 'A prayer to the sun'; 'Three Baroque meditations'; 'The Assisi fragments'; 'Ovid in the Third Reich'; 'History as poetry'; 'The imaginative life') and the uncollected 'Annunciations' (first published in *The Penguin Book of Contemporary Verse*, 1962.) The pamphlet's title (which is the Italian word for 'prayers') encapsulates not only the tones and moral vision of the poems included there but also that of the others Hill was to collect later for *King Log*, most of which were first published periodically in Jon Silkin's magazine, *Stand*. The TLS reviewer of *Preghiere* (25 August 1966) wrote that Hill had 'a disappointingly ingrown talent' and that his poems were 'mandarin and rarefied' offering 'a contrast to the earthy particularity of the others'. It is hard to see anything 'mandarin and rarefied' in such lines as 'I watch a slag/Scale the glinting pit-side/Of its own slime' ('Men are a mockery of angels'); 'maggots churning spleen/to milk' (Domaine public'), or in the phrase 'blood-embroiled souls' of the third stanza of 'History as poetry', their effectiveness centering in their very 'earthy particularity'. Jon Silkin in an introductory essay to Robert Shaw's anthology of modern poetry, *Flashpoint* (Arnold and Son, Leeds, 1964) writes that 'the way in which Geoffrey Hill's moral concern works is through his sensuousness, a sensuousness that is harsh, abrasive, translucent' (p.20).

From *Critical Quarterly* 4, vol. 20 (Winter 1978). Copyright © 1978 by Manchester University Press.

One can expand upon Silkin's insight and say that Hill's meticulous ordering of words, phrases and punctuation enacts a syntactical force comparable to that physical force it both conveys and attempts to transcend; the syntax serving as the physical means of embodying a powerful spiritual and intellectual integrity (whether it be Hill's own, or that vicariously bestowed upon the various 'personae' of his poems: e.g. the two respective poets, Tommasso Campanella and Robert Desnos, in 'Men are a mockery of angels' and 'Domaine public'). The conscious objectivity of the syntax conveys, through the art of poetry, the force of an inner vision which matches the unredeemed brutality of external reality:

> Anguish bloated by the replete scream.
> Flesh of abnegation: the poem
> Moves grudgingly to its extreme form,
> Vulnerable, to the lamp's fierce head
> Of well-trimmed light. In darkness outside
> Foxes and rain-sleeked stones and the dead—
> Aliens of my own blood—. . .
>   ('Three Baroque meditations': 2)

Just how crucial the least detail of syntax can be in a reading of Hill's poetry is illustrated by the fact that in the version of this poem in *King Log* there is a comma after 'outside' which makes one pause long enough to consider the tension of the poet's mind as he contemplates the juxtaposition of the bleak silence of reality and the inner 'voices' of his own thoughts. Writing of Yeats in his essay 'The conscious mind's intelligible structure' Hill says, 'It is as though the very recalcitrance of language—and we know that Yeats found the process of composition arduous—stood for the primary objective world in one of its forms of cruelty and indifference; but also for the cultivation of that other objectivity, won through toil.' In terms of Hill's own poetry the objectivity of 'the lamp's fierce head/Of well-trimmed light' (i.e. the rational poetic intelligence) is pitted against the inviolability of 'Foxes and rain-sleeked stones and the dead' (i.e. the unredeemed anarchy and arbitrariness of nature).

It is this balanced tension between art and reality which informs all the poems in *Preghiere* and *King Log* and enables Hill to say (again in the second of 'Three Baroque meditations'),

> For I am circumspect,
> Lifting the spicy lid of my tact
> To sniff at the myrrh.

By 'tact' Hill means the testing of his powers of moral and aesthetic discrimination through the selection and deployment of his poetic diction, without being insincere to the truth of his own imagination or the objective world which resides all around him. The self-tortuous balance is caught in the juxtaposition between the unanswered (because unanswerable) question:

> Do words make up the majesty
> Between the stones and the void?
> ('Three Baroque meditations': 1)

and (in the same poem) the ineluctable fact of

> An owl plunges to its tryst
> With a field-mouse in the sharp night.
> My fire squeals and lies still

where the innocent atrocities of nature co-exist with the crimes of fallen man (re-enacted in the 'fire' of the poet's imagination). For Hill, every poet has to forge his art out of intractable reality and, although he may evade the brutal facts of contemporary and historical reality (which Hill does not, of course) he still has to incorporate concrete images of that externality he is attempting to surmount into his poetry if he is to remain intelligible. The problem, of course, is not unique: in the late nineteenth century Mallarmé and the Symbolists had attempted to capture the essence of 'Le néant' in terms of abstraction in order to negate the demands of reality. Since that time poets have had great difficulty in finding a proper balance between the demands of the imagination and those of the world (Wallace Stevens's poetry, for instance, is founded—not wholly successfully, I feel—on the premises of the former; and, inversely, the poetry of MacNeice and Spender, for example, dealing literally—and often precariously—with the latter). In the case of Hill's poetry the poet believes that total abstraction is an ineffectual response because it neglects in its generalisation the unique aspects of the world, whereas absolute concern with concreteness negates the unifying power of the imagination: he prefers to adopt a 'tactful' balance between the two; unlike Donald Davie, for example, who can expound dogmatically that,

> It is my case against the symbolist theorists that, in trying to remove the human smell from poetry, they are only doing harm. For poetry to be great, it must reek of the human, as Wordsworth's poetry does.
> ('The reek of the human' in *Articulate Energy*, p.165)

In *King Log* Hill tests the 'reek' of humanity against the artifices of poetry and prayer, without renouncing either.

Jon Silkin, in the most intelligent and extensive essay yet on Hill's poetry, writes of Hills 'tact' as a quality of 'evasive caution' by which 'self-questioning exposes further recessions of self-doubts and questions'. Hill himself, however, has provided us with a better definition of it in his essay on the poetry of Jonathan Swift, 'The poetry of "reaction" (in *The World of Jonathan Swift: Essays for the Tercentenary,* collected and edited by Brian Vickers (Blackwell, 1968), pp. 165–212), where he describes Swift's 'preoccupation with verbal values' (p. 199) in terms of his 'creative tact' (p. 200) which is succinctly described as the ability of Swift's dramatic poetry 'to test various techniques against varying situations and successfully reduce a dangerous immediacy to a more remote hypothesis' (p. 201). In Swift's satire (Hill argues) the moral 'reaction' to the injustices of man and nature is couched in artistic terms which simultaneously assimilate the insensitive clichés of the language of a particular society and Swift's own sensitive awareness of that insensitivity: Hill quotes the famous lines from 'Verses on the death of Dr Swift' to support his thesis (p. 199),

> My female Friends, whose tender Hearts
> Have better learn'd to act their Parts
> Receive the News in doleful Dumps,
> 'The Dean is dead (and what is Trumps?)'

Hill argues that it is this power of Swift's 'to move with fluent rapidity from private to public utterance and from the formal to the intimate in the space of a few lines' which enables him to challenge satirically 'a sense of tradition and community . . . by a strong feeling for the anarchic and the predatory' (p. 196). In *King Log* tradition and community are tested thematically by the subject of war and persecution (e.g. the American Civil War in 'Locust songs'; the Wars of the Roses, specifically the Battle of Towton, in the sequence of eight unrhymed sonnets, 'Funeral music'; and the political imprisonment of the four poets Campanella, Hernandez, Desnos and Mandelshtam under four different tyrannical regimes, in the sequence 'Four poems regarding the endurance of poets') and syntactically by the intrusion of reality upon the 'remote hypothesis' or idealistic artifice of the poetry. In the following poem it is the contrast between the parenthesis of the speaking voice with its abstracted statements, and the intractable silence of the earth's concrete imagery which creates the tension between man's mortality and the earth's eternity; as well as 'placing', by the use of dramatic irony, the artifice of poetry against the objective facts of anarchy and predation:

> 'At noon,
> As the armies met, each mirrored the other;
> Neither was outshone. So they flashed and vanished

> And all that survived them was the stark ground
> Of this pain. I made no sound, but once
> I stiffened as though a remote cry
> Had heralded my name. It was nothing . . .'
> Reddish ice tinged the reeds; dislodged, a few
> Feathers drifted across; carrion birds
> Strutted upon the armour of the dead.
>
> ('Funeral music': 7)

The vision and language recall that of biblical exhortations on man's vanity, but throughout the sequence of eight sonnets there is no call to faith, only desperate questions which, by their very nature, are unanswerable. In the following example the two subjunctives 'if' set up an idealistic hypothesis whose fictional nature is amplified by the self-questioning tone of the final clause:

> If it is without
> Consequence when we vaunt and suffer, or
> If it is not, all echoes are the same
> In such eternity. Then tell me, love,
> How that should comfort us—or anyone
> Dragged half-unnerved out of this worldly place,
> Crying to the end 'I have not finished'.
>
> ('Funeral music': 8)

'Love' here conveys both the physical presence of a lover and that of the abstract spiritual quality, so it is both a direct question which is not answered by another, and a terrible self-communing (like a prayer) which opens up desperate wounds in the mind of this contemplative who has already examined Christian faith remorselessly ('When we chant/"Ora, ora pro nobis" it is not/Seraphs who descend to pity but ourselves' of sonnet five) and discovered the ultimate sterility of reason (the lines, 'an unpeopled region/ Of ever new-fallen snow, a palace blazing/With perpetual silence as with torches' of sonnet four, which recall, in terms of visual imagery, the scene of cruel indifference at the end of sonnet two, 'some trampled/Acres, parched, sodden or blanched by sleet,/Stuck with strange-postured dead', and prefigure the end of sonnet seven, 'Reddish ice tinged the reeds; dislodged, a few/Feathers drifted across; carrion birds/Strutted upon the armour of the dead').

In his short entry on Allen Tate (a poet whose influence on Hill has been considerable) in *The Concise Encyclopaedia of English and American Poets and Poetry* (Hutchinson, 1963, edited by D. Hall and S. Spender, pp. 302–3) Hill writes,

Tate's dominant preoccupations have largely centred upon the Civil War and its consequences. In an early prose work, *Stonewall Jackson* (1928), he ascribes to the antebellum South that 'historical sense of obligation' without which 'society becomes a chaos of self-interest' . . . Tate has suggested that this poem's ('Ode to the Confederate Dead') structure is 'the objective frame for the tension between the two themes, 'active faith' which has decayed, and the 'fragmentary cosmos' which surrounds us'. As a craftsman, Tate may be said to utter the 'formal pledge' of art in the presence of 'aimless power'; the poems are parables of this persistent opposition.

Hill's reading of Tate, and its crystallisation in this essay of 1963, finds a creative parallel in the poems of *King Log*, particularly in 'Funeral music', where (apart from a similar use of civil war as an analogue for both external and internal conflict) the characteristic tension between 'the "formal pledge" of art' and 'the presence of "aimless power" ' is most evident. In the appended essay to the sequence 'Funeral music', for example, Hill writes that he 'was attempting a florid grim music broken by grunts and shrieks' in a sequence which 'avoids shaping . . . characters and events into any overt narrative or dramatic structure. The whole inference, though, has value if it gives a key to the ornate and heartless music punctuated by mutterings, blasphemies and cries for help.' He also notes a contemporaneous writer's account of the Battle of Towton: 'The blood of the slain lay caked with the snow which covered the ground and that, when the snow melted, the blood flowed along the furrows and ditches for a distance of two or three miles.' Although this essay makes the poem no easier for the reader, it does indicate Hill's discursive intention of juxtaposing the images of the 'fragmentary chaos' ('a few feathers drifted across' from sonnet seven) against the ' "formal pledge" of art'—'(Suppose all reconciled/By silent music; imagine the future/Flashed back at us, like steel against the sun,/ Ultimate recompense)' from sonnet two, for example, whereby reality and idealism fuse within a tense collocation of imagistic and narrative material which Hill has borrowed eclectically from his studied reading of the characters and events of the Wars of the Roses. The 'potted' biographies of the three protagonists in the poem, Suffolk, Tiptoft and Rivers (which Hill provides in his essay on 'Funeral music') highlight the paradoxical nature of man prosaically ('Tiptoft, patron of humanist scholars, was known as the Butcher of England because of his pleasure in varying the accepted postures of judicial death') whilst their documented deeds and 'characters' are transformed imaginatively in the poem by Hill, and they serve him as a foundation upon which to explore poetically the eternal paradoxes of man: his capacity for meditation and action; idealism and realism; love and hate, and his individual predilection for mind or body (the contemplation of the place of the soul in this scheme is problematic: one of the unidentified protagonists saying, 'Let mind be more precious than soul; it will not/ Endure'—sonnet four). The conflict between such paradoxes is a central aspect of *King Log* and is crucial to the book's division into two sections of 'King Log' and 'King Stork'. This unifying pattern is also individually embodied in every poem in the volume: i.e., the poetic fusion of the differences existing between the meditative life of poetry and prayer ('Preghiere' and 'King Log') and the active life of decision and violence ('King Stork'). The title, *King Log,* comes from a fable by Aesop in which Zeus makes a log king of a pond, but this 'king' is jumped on and squatted upon by the frogs because he is too contemplative and easy-going. The frogs demand of Zeus a more active king and he sends a water-snake (King Stork) to govern them, and the snake devours all the frogs. We are told that 'This fable teaches us that we are better off with an indolent and harmless rules than with a mischief-making tyrant' (*Fables of Aesop,* translated by A. Handford, (Penguin 1954), p.44). Hill, of course, does not believe that the problem is to be solved so easily. The 'life of decision' in the volume is usually of a political nature, as is indicated by the quotation from Bacon's *Advancement of Learning* which serves as the book's epigraph: 'From moral virtue let us pass onto matter of power and commandment . . .'. The prose postscript, 'King Stork', aptly records the force of political violence in a coldly objective prose style (e.g. 'Suffolk . . . was in fact butchered across the gunwale of a skiff'). This discursiveness 'places' the recorded historical facts in a realm of reality, whilst the characteristically meditative syntax of the poems in the preceding section, 'King Log', are thus retrospectively seen to be of a fictional nature possessing reality only in the imagination of the poet. The 'attempted reparation' of the poem 'In memory of Jane Fraser' (a poem from the early 'fifties) possibly represents a decision on Hill's part to do 'violence' (of a necessary kind?) upon one of his own poems, in his revision of it. The 'realism' of the essay and the admission that he has had problems with that particular poem admits the reader into a realm of reality beyond the fictional world of the poems in 'King Log'; by the time we close the book it is uncertain to what extent 'the "formal pledge" of art' has redeemed the 'fragmentary cosmos', but like Keith Douglas's 'useless pity' for the dead (in *Alamein To Zem Zem),* Hill's poems exist in an intransitive relation to the 'aimless power' of the world: the 'remote hypothesis' of a poet's 'creative tact' never fully transcends the 'dangerous immediacy' of contemporary and historical reality.

JOHN NEEDHAM

The Idiom of
"Mercian Hymns"

Having thought it clear that stylistic
poise and subtlety were amongst the chief characteristics of Hill's *Mercian
Hymns*, I was somewhat jolted by Eric Homberger's saying that Hill, in
these poems, 'shifts levels of diction uncertainly, as though the colloquial
were about to explode in his face'. On the same page Homberger adds that
Poem XX, which refers to modern bungalows with names like 'Maldon', is
about 'the diminution of historic battles to suburban house-names'. Evidently a failure to take the subtlety of the idiom and a tendency to over-
simplify the attitudes go together. It is like the oversimplification that even
these days is sometimes inflicted on Pope's mock-heroics—'the epic past
played off against the trivial present', and so on. In fact, in Hill's art as in
Pope's, the relations between various historical phases and, correspondingly, between various idioms are complex and various. They are, indeed,
too complex to be reduced to any formula—though one can almost always
say that his surprising juxtapositions are creative (they issue, for instance,
in images) and that they turn 'wit' into an instrument of the historical
imagination.

Hill's wit, again like Pope's, can be described as the conscious and
simultaneous perception of similarity and difference. Pope, for instance,
develops the idea that, for all the differences, the removal of Arabella
Fermor's hair is like the removal of Helen from Troy; Hill, to take an
immediate example from the poem already referred to, describes the suburban houses as follows:

From *English* 131, vol. 28 (Summer 1979). Copyright © 1979 by the English Association.

Coiled entrenched England: brickwork and paintwork
stalwart above hacked marl. The clashing primary
colours—'Ethandune', 'Catraeth', 'Maldon',
'Pengwern'. Steel against yew and privet. Fresh
dynasties of smiths.

The *Henry V* set of feelings about the English as solid, vigorous and crude, which is implicit in 'stalwart', 'hacked', 'steel', and 'yew' (recalling the bow), is evoked by a contemplation of the style of suburbia. The contrast is, of course, mildly comic—the puns ensure that—but there are other factors. For instance, the context brings out the literal meaning of 'clashing', to suggest that modern crudity and ancient vigour are aspects of the same thing; and 'smiths' (Smiths) not only points to the particular sense in which we now live in the 'age of the common man' but also registers the notion that England always *was* chiefly the product of the common man. Further, the elements juxtaposed (old battles, new bungalows) are fused together and not merely held up for separate and ironic contemplation. There is obviously no way in which one can *show* that this is so; but one can at least note that the verbal texture is dense to the point of solidity. This is a matter of the implications of the words going fully and freely in both directions. For example, in 'steel against yew and privet', the first three words sound on the one hand like a ringing phrase about Agincourt; on the other they are, with a change of sense in the preposition ('against' meaning 'next to') a good image of close-trimming. If, further, one holds onto the more hostile sense of 'against', it implies that the trees are fighting back; which is a little joke—though the joke contains the point that even in suburban gardens there still *is* a fight against nature. This line of thought is carried on into 'privet' where, because of the conspicuously unheroic qualities of that shrub, the joke is broadened a little. Similarly with 'hacked' the literal sense, coming in from the battle context, is a little excessive, or so it seems, so that the English seem odd—'they are so comically violent that they even knock the soil about'. But 'hacked' is also exactly right for the look of that heavy clay when ploughed or dug. In a slightly different way but with a similar density of effect, 'paintwork' and 'brickwork' refer naturally to the modern context and also take on an Anglo-Saxon feel— as though work was spelled 'weorc'. One is, in short, allowed to dwell upon a large number of relevant implications. One might say, in fact, that Hill has a 'historical imagination' in an unusually full sense of the phrase; the density of his language, packed at different historical levels, is the sign of very fully imagined effects.

In this fusion of different levels of reference one gets, I think, three broad possibilities: first, a modern idiom with archaic undercurrents; second, a predominantly archaic idiom imposed on a modern context; and, third, a more equal blend of old and new; it is in the third group that the most striking and complex effects are reached. What follows are some commentaries on poems of each type made with the intention of showing a little of the flexibility and power of Hill's idiom. Perhaps I should first make the general comment that though many of the poems in the sequence are impressive considered alone they are not entirely free-standing, being marked by pressures and implications from other poems. I restrict myself to the more obvious points at which the following poems connect with the rest of the sequence.

Poem XIX is typical of those starting at the modern end of the scale:

> Behind the thorn-trees thin smoke, scutch-grass or
>   wattle smouldering. At this distance it is
>   hard to tell. Far cries impinge like the faint
>   tinking of iron.
>
> We have a kitchen-garden riddled with toy-shards,
>   with splinters of habitation. The children shriek
>   and scavenge, play havoc. They incinerate boxes,
>   rags and old tyres. They haul a sodden log, hung
>   with soft shields of fungus, and launch it upon
>   the flames.

This begins with a rather informal modern feeling, especially in the second sentence, and this is unobtrusively played off against the timeless air of the content, which evokes, as do other poems in the sequence, the bare essential, perennial features of the Mercian landscape. 'Tinking' also has two different time references; immediately, one takes it simply as a current onomatopoeic word, but then one feels behind it the old verb 'to tink', used of primitive ironworking. These feelings of the contemporary, the historic and the timeless combine to give that elusive air which is characteristic of many poems in the sequence. In this poem the words 'at this distance it is hard to tell' strike the keynote. It is a note on which the whole sequence ends, with a short poem about Offa the king (whom the poet tells us, in a note at the end, is 'the presiding genius of the West Midlands' from the eighth century until now):

> And it seemed, while we waited, he began to walk to-
>   wards us   he vanished
>   he left behind coins, for his lodging, and traces of
>   red mud.

This is a reminder that the history evoked in the sequence though rich and haunting is precarious. This atmosphere is generated by bringing to bear on history that sense of wonder which always tells you, to use Lawrence's phrase, 'you can't lay your mind on it'; and one of its most valuable effects here is to prevent the 'historical sense' from becoming, as it usually does, a mere grid of abstractions.

To return to Poem XIX; it continues, in the second paragraph, with a simple clipped movement; however, since the children feeding the garden fire are implicitly seen as re-creating a purification ritual, the simple repetitive movement itself takes on a slightly ritual feeling. Going along with double implications of the rhythm are other kinds of doubleness; as in phrases like 'splinters of habitation' and 'incinerate boxes' where Hill shows a Popean fondness for pairings of Latin and Old English derivatives; or, in a different way, in 'shriek and scavenge' where references to animals, savages and children are all easily accommodated. And this is perhaps the best place to note that Hill's recurrent images of layers of existence, deposited, buried and accumulated over great ages of development also applies to people themselves. In Poem XXII, for instance, there is an image of the poet as boy during a World War II air-raid, huddled in his 'earthy shelter', implicitly like a badger; and in a similar vein Offa says of himself, during his gestation, 'I was invested in mother-earth, the crypt of roots and endings'. This sense of everything, even abstractions like 'endings', partaking of the same mode of existence, is summed up in the image of the poet's garden in Poem XII, composed of 'Telluric cultures enriched with shards, corms, nodules, the sunk solids of gravity'. The doubleness of reference in Poem XIX, however, is finest in the closing image. It is double initially by virtue of being a metaphor—a metaphor with a beautiful surprise-element in the soft/hard contrast of shield and fungus, but it then takes on a further range of reference in the allusion to ship-burial. The allusion comes in so effortlessly that one is quietly convinced of the same-ness of the primitive and the contemporary, registering the difference only as an aesthetically attractive addition. To comment on the result rather than the process of this art: it is not the originality of any of Hill's insights into historiography that is valuable, but the poise with which he holds the relevant ones in play without blurring his images.

If we turn to the second sort of effect that I noted above (a primarily archaic idiom imposed on a modern context) we get broader and more obvious effects. Poem XXVI, for example, is a Jeremiad on the backslidings of the Mercians in which an Old English poetic manner is imposed on a modern post-Christmas-dinner scene:

> Fortified in their front parlours, at Yuletide men
> are the more murderous. Drunk, they defy battle-
> axes, bellow of whale-bone and dung.

> Troll-wives, groaners in sweetness, tooth-bewitchers,
>   you too must purge for the surfeit of England—
>   who have scattered peppermint and confetti, your
>   hundreds-and-thousands.

Though broad, however, the effects are just as rich as the more subtle ones at which we have been looking. For instance, 'tooth-bewitchers' condenses dental, sexual and magical implications; the phrase suggests 'they can put spells on your teeth', 'they are wonderful cooks', and 'you want to bite them'. The idiom of the poem is odd enough to have a distinctive individual feel, but at the same time the latent power of the words is released in what in the end is seen to be a quite natural way. 'Who have scattered peppermint and confetti', for example, is surprising because of the disparity between the grim, high Anglo-Saxon manner and the extreme un-Anglo-Saxon-ness of the content; but one also notes the element of justice in the effect, since peppermint and confetti really are symbols of profusion and luxury, and Hill makes the reader *feel* this—he brings the tired words back to life. Further, I think, the felt delight in the richness of the language corresponds with a delight in the richness of the history itself—the two are felt to be aspects of the same thing.

In this group one has poems in which the atmosphere is very different—Poem XXV, for example, which is an elegy for the poet's grandmother and, I think, one of the best poems in the sequence:

> Brooding on the eighteenth letter of *Fors Clavigera,*
>   I speak this in memory of my grandmother, whose
>   childhood and prime womanhood were spent in the
>   nailer's darg.
>
> The nailshop stood back of the cottage, by the fold.
>   It reeked stale mineral sweat. Sparks had furred
>   its low roof. In dawn-light the troughed water
>   floated a damson-bloom of dust—
>
> not to be shaken by posthumous clamour. It is one
>   thing to celebrate the 'quick forge', another
>   to cradle a face hare-lipped by the searing wire.
>
> Brooding on the eighteenth letter of *Fors Clavigera,*
>   I speak this in memory of my grandmother, whose
>   childhood and prime womanhood were spent in the
>   nailer's darg.

The poem is the most direct and emotional in the sequence and contains no verbal fireworks, the stylistic subtlety being almost entirely in movement and manner. It opens on a rather informal conversational note (line one) and moves quickly into a more formal rhythm (line two), which then turns into a fourteener with dialect vocabulary (lines three and four). The second paragraph might be described as plain modern poetic style moving, in the last sentence, into a slightly more elevated manner from which the poet can get into the high-toned irony of the start of the third paragraph before coming back down into the looser structure of the sentence that follows. Despite the obvious differences I put this with Poem XXVI because the high style in the first paragraph sounds the ground-note from which all the rest is a departure. The poem exists at a point where various idioms—traditional poetic, new poetic, dialect, current speech—meet, and the poet is implicitly claiming for himself, in being able to command this medium, the right to speak on English social and historical development; the style is the guarantee of the inwardness.

To turn now to our third group, Poem XIV is one where old and new idioms are more equally mixed. This is another poem dealing with Offa who here appears as a mixture of ancient autocrat and modern bureaucrat; as in other poems, he is, though clever and imaginative, rather vain, solitary and mean:

> Dismissing reports and men, he put pressure on the
> wax, blistered it to a crest. He threatened male-
> factors with ash from his noon cigar.

> When the sky cleared above Malvern, he lingered in
> his orchard; by the quiet hammer-pond. Trout-fry
> simmered there, translucent, as though forming the
> water's under-skin. He had a care for natural min-
> utiae. What his gaze touched was his tenderness.
> Woodlice sat pellet-like in the cracked bark and
> a snail sugared its new stone.

> At dinner, he relished the mockery of drinking his
> family's health. He did this whenever it suited
> him, which was not often.

The greater subtlety of the medium in this group corresponds, of course, with a greater subtlety and penetration of content. Take, for instance, the pattern of burning metaphors and references. In the simmering trout-fry the juxtapositions of the quiet beauty of the scene and the references to cooking seem at first sight rather grotesque—and indeed they are; but they also feel natural, because 'simmering', as well as having a sinister allusion to holocaust, is also exactly right for the fish just under the surface so that a vivid image is produced. 'Quiet hammer-pond' is similar. The surprise of the quiet/hammer clash is naturalised by the reminder that water truly has enormous latent power—the pond itself seems to possess an explosive force (here too there is, of course, a sense of burning somewhere behind 'hammer'). The natural feel of the poetic effects makes the content also feel natural—that is, the inner violence is seen to be as much a part of nature as the surface beauty; and the same pent-up force is present in the character of Offa himself. To take that last point a little further one needs to refer to the epigraph to *Mercian Hymns* which Hill takes from C. H. Sisson and which includes Blackstone's dictum that all human laws depend on 'the law of nature and the law of revelation'; Hill illuminates this with a sustained insight into the intricate connections of the human with the natural—we will look later at the religious aspect of the sequence. It seems to me, incidentally, that Jon Silkin, in his essay on Hill, gets a little out of touch with Hill's art in his comments on this poem; he suggests that the 'ash' of the first paragraph refers to Auschwitz, but it seems to me more likely to refer to Hiroshima. A nuclear allusion is almost built into the word 'ash' these days and 'noon cigar', I would say, refers to the fact that the bomb was dropped at that time of day and was, of course, that shape. The rather grotesque nature of these double-meanings is typical of the art of the whole poem.

So far as techniques goes Poem XVII belongs, I think, in the same group as that last one, but the atmosphere is completely different. Here the juxtapositions are more obviously brilliant and the comedy has a lighter note:

> He drove at evening through the hushed Vosges. The
> car radio, glimmering, received broken utterance
> from the horizon of storms . . .

> 'God's honour—our bikes touched; he skidded and came
> off.' 'Liar.' A timid father's protective bellow.
> Disfigurement of a village-king. 'Just look at
> the bugger . . .'

> His maroon GT chanted then overtook. He lavished on
> the high valleys its *haleine*.

Jon Silkin says that he is uncertain about the second paragraph of this poem so I had better offer my own suggested interpretation before commenting on the style. As I understand it, Offa, the time of day and the weather rather ominous, is driving through Europe and finds himself behind another car which he wants to overtake. He suddenly recollects a childhood incident in which he knocked another child from a bike and was beaten by the child's father. The memory causes an eruption of aggressive feeling;

he puts his foot down, blows the horn and overtakes with a roar. As in other poems the figure of Offa evidently includes the personality of the poet himself. A variety of historical strands are woven into the immediate situation; the current (the GT), the larger scale of modern history ('horizon of storms'), the medieval (in 'haleine', which Hill explains in a note), the pre-historic ('village-king'), the pre-human ('bellow') and, in the Wordsworthian power of the 'broken utterance', the pre-animal. The play of the diction between these levels is beautifully managed. 'Broken utterance', for instance, is obviously right for Nature's prophecies, mysterious and tragic, and is successfully applied to radio noise (for which it might easily have seemed *too* exalted) because, as usual, there is a valid point behind the fun—here it is a point about the mystery of radio and the way in which crucial modern events have been bound up with radio broadcasts. (In Poem XXII, about childhood during World War II, one finds: 'The wireless boomed its commands. I loved the battle-anthems and the gregarious news.') In the third paragraph Hill's art is pushed, I think, to its limit. The allusion in 'haleine' is to Roland's horn; Hill gives the line 'Co dist le reis: Cel corn ad lunge aleine', which is translated by Scott Moncrieff as ' "That horn", the king says, "hath a mighty strain" '. The richness of the word-play and the exuberance of the assonances again bring Pope to mind, and with him a phrase which I think Eliot was the first to use—albeit of Dryden—'creative satire'. Where, as in Dryden's Zimri or Pope's Atossa, the target is fully created as well as criticised, the art comes, after all the laughter or even bitterness, out of a sheer delight in, or love for, the thing itself. Perhaps one could call it the aesthetic aspect of the rule that one should condemn the vice and not the man. In this case there is no doubt about the poet's attitude to the vice—that sort of aggressive ego is a pollutant—but the rhythm and the imagery partake of the joy of superbia.

The finest single effect of this type, where the diverse elements both of style and content are most fantastically blended, is perhaps to be found in Poem XXVII, which is about the death of Offa:

> 'Now when King Offa was alive and dead', they were
>   all there, the funereal gleemen: papal legate and
>   rural dean; Merovingian car-dealers, Welsh mercen-
>   aries; a shuffle of house-carls.
>
> He was defunct. They were perfunctory. The ceremony
>   stood acclaimed. The mob received memorial vouch-
>   ers and signs.

> After that shadowy, thrashing mid-summer hail-storm,
> Earth lay for a while, the ghost-bride of livid
> Thor, butcher of strawberries, and the shire-tree
> dripped red in the arena of its uprooting.

The close of this, with its blend of mythological revival, realistic image and joke seems to me to be a magnificent success. It is, of course, the play of the first two paragraphs that makes 'butcher of strawberries' possible without disrupting the tone. The phrase is not merely a conceit; it conveys with peculiar precision the sense of the red flesh of the strawberries exposed after the storm has knocked the plants about. The joke-element, of course, works back from 'butcher' to 'livid' giving the latter word not only a colour value but the rather exaggerated colloquial sense ('He was *livid*') which makes Thor an angry bloke as well as a Norse deity.

The deities of Mercia are, of course, important in Hill's whole project, and this is perhaps a good point at which to say something more generally about this aspect of the poems. The following (from Poem XVI) resembles the Thor passage in that it also revives an ancient religious feeling by anchoring it firmly to a vivid image of perennial Mercia:

> Shafts from the winter sun homing upon earth's rim.
> Christ's mass: in the thick of the snowy forest the
> flickering evergreen fissured with light.

This is a reminder of other great religious developments in Mercia and the image, though it hasn't the brilliance of the lines about Thor, is, I think, impressively solid. In a different vein, Poem XXIV reminds us that the *official* images were not, even in the great age of religion, always effective; the medieval mason is said to 'pester upon tympanum and chancel arch his moody testament, confusing warrior with lion, dragon coils, tendrils of the stony vine'. In his case the vine *was* stony. All in all, I think, Hill has a measure of success in expressing religious feeling in terms of specific traditions and places and suggesting that the development has not been merely a tale of loss. But the effort sometimes seems to exist only at the level of bright idea, as, I think, in Poem III:

> On the morning of the crowning we chorused our re-
> mission from school. It was like Easter: hankies
> and gift-mugs approved by his foreign gaze, the
> village-lintels curlered with paper flags.
>
> We gaped at the car-park of 'The Stag's Head' where a
> bonfire of beer-crates and holly-boughs whistled

> above the tar. And the chef stood there, a king in
> his new-risen hat, sealing his brisk largesse with
> 'any mustard?'

Not to be too heavy-handed about this light, and delightful, poem, but I'm not sure that the whimsicality of the various religious references is entirely admirable. Still, those fancies are at least in the poet's own mind; in Poem XXI he tries to put fancies which, though not specifically religious, are similar in that they are of a past living in the imagination of the present, into the minds of folk off on a chara trip to Arthurian country:

> Tea was enjoyed by lakesides where
> all might fancy carillons of real Camelot vib-
> rating through the silent water.

It is, of course, beautifully done, but a bit too poetic to convince me that this is what the people really felt. The general point emerging from this applies, I think, also to the religious aspect of the sequence; the continuities of which Hill gives such solid images and subtle accounts are very much those of a poet; of continuities more embedded in the life of the community or in the popular imagination I don't think that Hill has much command.

I believe that his whole attempt is extraordinarily successful, however, and that even his relative failures are very instructive. To summarize the points that have been made here and there; Hill's idiom makes for very good writing about history. It enables him simultaneously to present several different views; that 'human nature is always and everywhere the same', as Johnson used to put it; that everything changes, and that history goes in cycles. And Hill's imagination is almost always strong enough to prevent the witty balance of these possibilities from degenerating into mere conceitedness. The reader always senses, moreover, the poet's conscious delight in the exercise of both wit and imagination, which implies, partly, a degree of self-confidence, as though the poet is saying 'See, my mind can live in some style with this apparently disparate cultural fragmentation'; partly it is a function of the imaginative sense of wonder which is particularly valuable here as an antidote against the confident and sterile abstractionism to which historiography is so often prone.

MERLE BROWN

"Funeral Music"

To note the indirectness of "Funeral Music" may be a step towards discovering the centrality to all of Hill's later sequences of the conviction, which he shares with Coleridge, that "meditation is central to practice." This discovery will prove most profitable if it is also recognized that Hill is not referring to thoughtful preparation for action or to brooding over events after they have occurred, but to meditation which is simultaneous with action.

Complaints concerning Hill's indirectness, as though it were a poetic weakness, usually stem from a neglect of this commitment on his part to the oneness of thought and action. C. H. Sisson, for example, in reacting to the two-page essay Hill appended to the eight poems of "Funeral Music," says:

> I find these explanations curious, and perhaps see them as more significant than they are. They seem to imply a notion of the sequence as artifact, as something worked towards the built, which suggests a growing distance between the poetic impulse and the words which finally appear on the page—a gain in architectonics, perhaps, but at a price which is so often paid, by all but the greatest writers, in a loss of immediacy. This is no more than a suspicion of what—as I see it—would be an unfortunate direction.

That is, however, the direction Sisson thinks Hill has moved in, for of *Mercian Hymns* (published in 1971, four years after "Funeral Music" first appeared, in Jon Silkin's *Stand*), he asks: "Is the choice of prose a mark of growing deliberation and a gap between the conception and the perfor-

From *Double Lyric: Divisiveness and Communal Creativity in Recent English Poetry.* Copyright © 1980 by Carolyn Brown. Columbia University Press.

mance?" And Hill's more recent sequence, "Lachrimae" in *Tenebrae* (London: André Deutsch, 1978), Sisson refers to "as indicating another mode for this singularly direct mind which, none the less, seems impelled to seek indirect utterance." For Sisson, immediacy and directness go along with a sense of experience, including poetic experience, as a flowing process rather than a human action; even Hill's indirection and meditativeness are spoken of as something to which Hill is "impelled." Great poetry, for Sisson, is unclogged verbal flow, an unimpeded stream between impulse and performance. For poetry like Hill's, in which human making, like all practice, achieves excellence only if impeded, clogged, and disrupted by hard thinking, Sisson's notion of poetry as process cannot but be an obstruction which makes the immediacy of the mediation of "Funeral Music" seem indirect to his thought-free viewing.

It is a different sort of directness which Jon Silkin is missing when he says that Hill found a way "to incarcerate the reader, and perhaps the writer also, in an inescapable response," but this method fails "to release him from a pre-occupation where the event has been so internalised that there results more response than event itself." The longer sequences require some "developed structure," Silkin grants, but Hill unfortunately "meets the problem without conceding to narrative a function it might usefully fulfil in his work," because, it would seem he prefers "internal impulsions" to "dramatic action." Of "Funeral Music" itself, Silkin says:

> the battle of Towton, and its murderousness, is not encapsulated as dramatic action, but brooded on after the event, thereby allowing the external state of the field and the state of the mind experiencing and responding to it to meet. It is the self-questioning, the doubts, the beliefs half-held with a conviction of personal honesty, the motives and the state of the spirit, that interest Hill, rather than the shaping action of narrative. Nevertheless, these things too have their form of collision with other minds, and through action, alter and are altered. And they could also, I feel, build a narrative unity that Hill has only tentatively, if at all, used.

With his modernistic bias, Sisson is impelled to regret the absence of a direct, psychic flow; Silkin, with his Marxist bias, misses a direct, objective flow, a collision of forces within an established setting. For him, a poem is a strategy by means of which the poet imprisons or captivates the citizen, forcing him to respond in a determined way, and then releases him, purging him of preoccupations and anxieties so that he can function properly and healthfully. Such directness or immediacy, though it may require much thought of a strategic nature prior to the experience of the poem itself, calls for an absence of thought in that experience totally at odds with Hill's sense not just of poetic experience, but also of human excellence, whether in primarily active or primarily meditative behavior.

Hill's sequences, and especially "Funeral Music," on which I intend to focus, succeed in the light of their own difficult conception. They should not be read as lyrical, as impulse bodied forth in words, or as narrative, as an "accumulating and continuous action." They are double lyrics or dramatic lyrics and are more authentic, closer to the way thoughtful, engaged human beings actually behave, than anything of a self-expressive nature can be, or anything that can be staged objectively or theatrically. It is not enough, moreover, to think of "Funeral Music" as a meeting of subject and object, as Silkin does when he says that Hill has written the poem so as to allow "the external state of the field and the state of the mind experiencing and responding to it to meet." For that notion blanks out what is most striking about these poems, that they are polycentric, including as part of them more than one originative center. Beyond presenting a scene or any "illusion of reality," they, first of all, implicate the act of their making by Hill himself. Furthermore, having recognized that this gives him as maker a special privilege not possessed by any of his antagonists within the scene or field of his making, Hill strives to double the poems, so that one scene is always more than one, not only that constituted by him as maker and including his antagonist, but also that which his antagonist constitutes and which includes him. The peculiar result of this is that when a reader slides, as is apt to happen, into taking a line in only one way, he feels the line being pulled away from him, or at least blurring, doubling up, so that he must check his glasses or rest his eyes. It is as though, as one viewed *Othello*, he also attended to Othello's constituting a drama that encompasses Iago and Shakespeare as they have encompassed him in their dramas; as if Anna, behind the words, is writing out a world which includes Levin and Tolstoy as she is included in their world; as though, as one reads *Women in Love,* he is also reading a second novel, *Men in Love,* written by Ursula-Frieda. Impulse and word, mind and field, these models simply do not touch the sharp-edged magnificence towards which Hill strives even in his finest short poems, but especially in his recent sequences.

Because these sequences are so dense, so multi-layered, so polyphonic, it is hard to say anything that is more than partly true of them. Even such a concession, moreover, is only partly true, for the uniqueness of these poems is beyond the reach of linguistic, structural analysis, by means of which intricacies can be shown, but not power, not explosiveness, not anguish, and not insight. These poems are genuine dramas, each line being vied for by opponents each of whom is a charged source of the line itself, so that it tends to double up disrelatedly, the linkage, the oneness so vividly and livingly unique as to exceed not just one's language but almost one's capacities for experiencing. I shall try to simplify without falsifying, beginning with the first poem of "Funeral Music," Hill's first major sequence:

> Processionals in the exemplary cave,
> Benediction of shadows. Pomfret. London.
> The voice fragrant with mannered humility,
> With an equable contempt for this World,
> 'In honorem Trinitatis'. Cash. The head
> Struck down into a meaty conduit of blood.
> So these dispose themselves to receive each
> Pentecostal blow from axe or seraph,
> Spattering block-straw with mortal residue.
> Psalteries whine through the empyrean. Fire
> Flares in the pit, ghosting upon stone
> Creatures of such rampant state, vacuous
> Ceremony of possession, restless
> Habitation, no man's dwelling-place.

The poem may be recognized as setting forth quite objectively the nature of the lives and deaths of the three men in whose memory "Funeral Music" is written, Suffolk (beheaded 1450), Worcester (beheaded 1470), and Rivers (beheaded 1483). They were Christian Neo-Platonists, viewing this world as a cave, this life as a procession of shadows. It is a no-man's land, a place to leave, especially since the death of the body is the release of the soul into a life of beatific immortality, its flight accompanied by the sound of psalteries "through the empyrean."

But the poet-historian who observes also judges these soldier-martyrs, with a contempt the equal of their contempt for this world. The word "vacuous" brings his dismissive judgment to the forefront. For the soldier-martyrs themselves, the word has to do with the emptying of the worldly, bodily aspect of the ceremony as the soul is possessed by way of a seraph and escorted to heaven. For the poet the word means that the whole show is a monstrous sham. The dualism of these Christians is just an elaborate excuse for their being so brutal, for their killing and being killed in this violent way. Each line should be read not just within its Christian framework, but also within that of the poet-historian, who would pull these "creatures of such rampant state," rampant as beasts of prey, but also as souls ready to spring into heavenly ghostliness, back into the flesh shockingly, with such lines as "Struck down into a meaty conduit of blood" and "Spattering block-straw with mortal residue." Repulsive it is, and their doubling their sight, believing the blow delivered by seraph as well as by axe, softened what they saw and so encouraged both victim and persecutor to take part, equally, in what was not at all the masquerade they took it to be.

However, reading the poem with an ear for the poet's sarcasm (to be heard clearly at least from the word "mannered" in line three on), one senses a growing worry on Hill's part over the similarity between the way he is dismissing the dualistically conceived lives of the soldier-martyrs and the way they dismissed the worldly aspects of their lives. For instance, the string of dismissive phrases with which the poem ends rises away from that pit not just spatially, but also temporally, not just toward the empyrean, but also toward the present, toward that comfortable dwelling-place which is the poet-historian's study, where he remains above action, meditatively. Thus, the string of phrases meant to free the poet from the murderous tangle of his subjects (the freedom to be self-righteous which Silkin missed in the sequence) actually entangles the poet in the very mesh he was using to entangle those subjects. Experienced doubly, that is, the string of phrases reveals the poet as observer and judge to be observed and judged. He uses his professional distinction between himself as observer and his subjects as the observed to escape the truth about his predicament just as his subjects used their religious distinction between soul and body to make their escape. In the short poem "History as Poetry," also to be found in *King Log*, Hill articulates his sense that a poetry which resuscitates the dead can avoid moral condemnation only by subjecting itself to such self-questioning that its primary form becomes self-condemnatory. The first poem of "Funeral Music" exceeds the reach of that poem by bringing the dead back to life in such a way that they observe and judge the very poet-historian who has exhumed, observed, and judged them. Thus chastened, Hill earns a truly liberating release from that reprehensible predicament of staring at another person whose eyes are closed, the predicament next to unavoidable by not just historians, but almost all observers. Though he cannot live by the Christian prescription, "Judge not . . . ," Hill attains a comparable innocence by way of experience, creating a poem-world in which he is judged as he judges, seen as he sees.

Although "Processionals in the exemplary cave" allows for the reading just given, it may not by itself require it. What makes the reading necessary—and this sort of thing is true of the sequence as a whole and of Hill's other sequences—is the gap between that first poem and the poem which follows it, "For whom do we scrape our tribute of pain?" Hill's move from the "they" and the implicit "one" of the first poem to the "we" which colors the second pervasively is what makes one stall uncertainly in the inaudible, invisible gap between the poems. One will connect with the developmental impulse in that gap and, as a result, read the first poem as suggested above, so that he experiences even in it the transformation of "one" and "they" to "we" and thus feels the rightness of the "we" of the first line of the second poem, only, I think, as he recognizes that the basic drama of "Funeral Music" is a combat between two forms of history, two ways of relating oneself as contemporary poet-historian to the past. The unheard way, which works silently behind the poem the actuality of which one is following and which presses everywhere against that actuality, is T. S. Eliot's way.

Even though Eliot observed that the trouble with the *Cantos* is that Pound's hells are always "for the other people" he conceives of the past as occurring without understanding, as in need of the poet-historian, who redeems it by giving it a new form within his understanding. Event and understanding, action and thought, soul and intellect—and this even in the *Four Quartets*—are, for all but the martyr-saint and the poet-historian, essentially separate. The martyr-saint, like the poet-historian, is utterly objective, impersonal, at one with God as Truth, as intellect. He achieves impersonality, which is what Beckett, in *Murder in the Cathedral,* means by losing one's will in God, finding "freedom in submission to God." The saint, that is, like the historian, is free of the laws determining history as an object of study. When Beckett is insisting that the priests unbar the door so that the knights may murder him, he condemns them for arguing

> by results, as the world does,
> To settle if an act be good or bad.
> You defer to the fact. For every life and every act
> Consequence of good and evil can be shown.
> And as in time results of many deeds are blended
> So good and evil in the end become confounded.
> It is not in time that my death shall be known;
> It is out of time that my decision is taken
> [. . .]
> I give my life
> To the Law of God above the Law of Man.

As objective poet-historian, as playwright, as a man who has given himself up to a perfect understanding of past events, Eliot is at one with the single point of awareness within the flux of the past which can be called supra-temporal, that of the martyr-saint. As a result, Eliot has no interest in the facts of Beckett's worldly life, the "meagre records" with which he says

Tennyson tampered "unscrupulously." His soul as historian, like Beckett's as saint, has become impersonally objective, at one with Intellect as "absolute law," "sufficient grace." For them alone, belief and understanding, soul and intellect, are absolutely identical. The rest of us, in contrast, the priests, the knights, the audience of the play, who live by the Law of Man, are radically flawed.

The subject of *Murder in the Cathedral* is the martyr-saint as set against "you others," mainly the soldier-knights, who are used as our representatives. There is no such split in "Funeral Music." In his essay appended to the sequence, Hill emphasizes that of the three soldiers in whose memory the poem was written, two were soldier-poets and the third was "patron of humanist scholars" in addition to being "the Butcher of England." Although their behavior seems more remote from Hill's than Beckett's from Eliot's, and, as much as Hill strives to reach an Eliotic position outside the "murderousness" of their lives, he is forced, both in his mortality and in his evasiveness, to accept his oneness with them. Action and meditation are at one. He is no better than they are.

They are, moreover, as good as he is, from which inference the second poem of the sequence proceeds:

> For whom do we scrape our tribute of pain—
> For none but the ritual king? We meditate
> A rueful mystery; we are dying
> To satisfy fat Caritas, those
> Wiped jaws of stone. (Suppose all reconciled
> By silent music; imagine the future
> Flashed back at us, like steel against sun,
> Ultimate recompense.) Recall the cold
> Of Towton on Palm Sunday before dawn,
> Wakefield, Tewkesbury: fastidious trumpets
> Shrilling into the ruck; some trampled
> Acres, parched, sodden or blanched by sleet,
> Stuck with strange-postured dead. Recall the wind's
> Flurrying, darkness over the human mire.

The soldier-poets are granted the meditativeness of the poet-historian as he is given an active involvement in their death and dying. The distinction between them as dead and him as living is erased so that the observations, the Neo-Platonic hopes, and the acidic doubts are all fused as part of the experience of the "us" of the poem. Because of the firm oneness of the poem, its doubleness is so delicate as to be almost inarticulable. Even in its unarticulated light, however, the crudeness which results from Eliot's splitting apart of action (that of the knights) and meditation (Beckett's

and his own) is made harshly apparent. Nonetheless, the poem is double
and needs to be read two ways at once. One way emphasizes the desperate
desolation of the worldly battle, the worthlessness of all it involved, unless
it was undergone with "an equable contempt," as is implicit in the phrase
"fastidious trumpets/ Shrilling into the ruck," a phrase that points to that
image of beatific redemption imagined in lines six and seven, "the future/
Flashed back at us, like steel against sun,/ Ultimate recompense." The way
of reading that doubles this blames the desolation on the beatific image,
and insists that the desolation, the trampled acres, are the only reality,
and the paradisal image for which one sacrifices his worldly self destructively
is truly a monstrous, illusory fancy, "fat Caritas, those/ Wiped jaws of stone."
There is, furthermore, a sense of how much alike beatific atonement and
the desolation of utter loss are. The last sentence, "Recall the wind's/
Flurrying, darkness over the human mire," which seems an awful judgment
on the meaninglessness of the Battle of Towton and the lives and deaths
it engulfed has an element of awesome mystery in its hushed silence which
seems at one with the beatific "Suppose all reconciled/ By silent music."
There is a touch of that peace that passed understanding in the way the
poem ends, just as there is a touch of arbitrary destructiveness in the
"reconciled/ By silent music," because it is preceded by the slightly frivolous
"Suppose" and then followed by an appositive image which with its
"Flashed" and "steel against sun" sounds harsh, aggressive, and militant,
even if the "ultimate recompense." Curiously, the angelic, the heavenly,
music is harsher ("fastidious trumpets") than its worldly counterpart, "the
wind's/ Flurrying."

The movement of "Funeral Music" is, thus, linear, developmental,
sequential. There is a momentous thrust forward between the first and
second poems; the second bears the first with it and yet grows beyond it
in the subtlety and delicacy of its onenesses and its divisivenesses. and yet,
though the individual poems do not move as sonnets—in which sestet
follows octet and yet must be experienced as simultaneous with it—the
sequence as a whole does work in just that way. One reads the second poem
as building on the first and going beyond it, but once one has done that,
he cannot return to the first poem and feel and respond to it as containing
what he had discovered as the essential, silent combat of the gap, that
between Hill and Eliot, and also the mysterious doubleness that pervades
the communal oneness of the second poem.

Consider, for instance, the phrase "Psalteries whine through the
empyrean," which read at this point will doubtless seem the very heart of
the first poem. It is an unavoidable evasive movement toward heaven,

following upon the anguishing repulsiveness of "Spattering block-straw with mortal residue," which one really does not want to contemplate at all. It echoes these two lines from "Little Gidding," which open the Dantesque "dead patrol" episode:

> After the dark dove with the flickering tongue
> Had passed below the horizon of his homing

The movement of Eliot's lines is in accord with his form of history; it is a movement of disengagement from the worldly and temporal. The "dark dove" is a fighter bomber on the way to being the Holy Ghost, the one destructive in an earthly way, the other, though also snakelike with its "flickering tongue," destructive for salvation. Hill's lines are implicated in the same movement, from spattered block-straw to empyrean. But the word "whine" adds a movement, drags the fleeing ghost back into its flesh, which marks all the difference between Eliot and Hill. The ascent is a movement of craven self-pity, even though twanged out on psalteries. Moreover, especially with Eliot's "dark dove" fighter bomber evoked, one cannot but recall "The nasal whine of power whips a new universe" from "Cape Hatteras," and, with that recall, he will also recognize that Hill's judgment of this *poésie des departs* is not at all Eliot's (who felt that by way of it Baudelaire glimpsed beatitude), but is much the same as Crane's

> Seeing himself an atom in a shroud—
> Man hears himself an engine in a cloud!

Sensing his small empty worthlessness, man soars heavenward as an aeronaut. Crane has been scorned for lauding modern technology in its expansive conquest of space. Like Hill, he did, it is true, sympathize with that effort because he recognized the authenticity of the need behind it; but, also like Hill, Crane felt the emptiness of the effort (to be sensed even in the "engine in a cloud," which, because of the clanging rhyme with "shroud," is felt to be indistinguishable from the "atom in a shroud"), so that he insisted that the flight must be curved back earthward, or else it will turn back of its own accord in an uncontrollably destructive way.

"Funeral Music" is held together not by a narrative line or by recurrent imagery, but by problems in the relationship between the poet-historian and his subject, the soldier-poets. Even though it seems magnificent when read as both sequential and simultaneous, it is always edged with a problem in painful need of solution, so that it does not move like a broad and deep river, but twists and turns, swerves or shrinks. If, for instance, their oneness, their being a "we," is implicit in the "one" and "they" of the first poem, the unison of the "we" of the second is ruffled by a latent doubleness. The "we" of that poem is not an achieved oneness which is then sustained for the rest of the sequence. Indeed, it is immediately broken by the sarcasm with which the third poem opens: "They bespoke doomsday and they meant it by/ God." Even more striking that poem is made up of four quite discrete voices, ranging from a modern voice that dismisses the whole bloody mess with " 'Oh, that old northern business . . .' " to a voice spoken from the field itself, at the end of the battle: "Blindly the questing snail, vulnerable/ Mole emerge, blindly we lie down . . ."

In response to such disintegrative cacophony, the fourth poem is Hill's single, mortal combat with Averroes, who would put an end to conflict by collapsing all diversity into a single identity, that of the mind, the Intellect, as "absolute law," "sufficient grace." Speaking in his own, single voice, Hill refuses to reject the world as a "waste history" or "void rule"; arguing against any sort of Eliotic fusion of soul with intellect and against structuralist reductions of individual men to anonymous Language, he insists on his own identity, on the inviolability of his soul, and with his single voice he is arguing for us all. The gentle, isolate beauty of the fourth poem is drowned out at once, however, by the large, common "we" voice which speaks the whole of the fifth poem. This "we" begins by echoing the last line of the fourth poem, to show that it thinks of itself as in entire accord with Hill. At the start, at least all Christians are meant to be included in its "we"; but by the end it is clearly excluding from its "we" all its opponents, who of course are to be thought of as "the damned." Indeed, as the poem ends, it is affirming the unison of its "we" while enjoying the howls of those it is torturing to death,

> Those righteously-accused those vengeful
> Racked on articulate looms indulge us
> With lingering shows of pain, a flagrant
> Tenderness of the damned for their own flesh:

The colon with which the poem ends and the way the sixth begins

> My little son, when you could command marvels
> Without mercy, outstare the wearisome
> Dragon of sleep, I rejoiced above all—
> A stranger well-received in your kingdom.

indicate that one of "the damned" is speaking the sixth poem (he addresses his own flesh tenderly with "My little son") and that he is no more or less partisan than the inflated "we" of the fifth poem, whom Hill pricked sharply with his use of "righteously-accused" in place of "rightly-accused."

Hill's closeness to the dying soldier-poet of the sixth poem is con-
firmed by the seventh poem, which is a duet between Hill and another
soldier-poet, whose sense of himself is the same as that of the soldier-poet
of the sixth poem. The voice in quotation marks is that of the soldier, who
died in the Battle of Towton and who wins our admiration by judging
himself, his life, and the murderous behavior of the armies, with both of
which he identifies his existence, as damnable and abandoned to oblivion.
The other voice is that of the impersonal, modern poet-historian, who by
way of images presented objectively concurs harshly and objectionably with
the judgment of the self-condemning soldier:

> Reddish ice tinged the reeds; dislodged, a few
> Feathers drifted across; carrion birds
> Strutted upon the armour of the dead.

This conclusion to the poem fixes fearfully the sense that the men who
fought at Towton are of no more consequence or value than carrion birds.
When the armies met, at noon, "each mirrored the other;/ Neither was
outshone." At the end, their armor mirrors the carrion birds, which strut
as they strutted. The dislodged feathers may be from the helmets of the
dead or from the carrion birds; it is a matter of indifference.

The eighth and last poem tends to evaporate vaguely unless it is
read in close relation with the end of the seventh.

> Not as we are but as we must appear,
> Contractual ghosts of pity; not as we
> Desire life but as they would have us live,
> Set apart in timeless colloquy:
> So it is required; so we bear witness,
> Despite ourselves, to what is beyond us,
> Each distant sphere of harmony forever
> Poised, unanswerable. If it is without
> Consequence when we vaunt and suffer, or
> If it is not, all echoes are the same
> In such eternity. Then tell me, love,
> How that should comfort us—or anyone
> Dragged half-unnerved out of this worldly place,
> Crying to the end 'I have not finished'.

Especially as it ends, the seventh poem has the narrowest and most fierce
focus of the entire sequence. The very rhythm of its last line affects one
like sharp blows on the chest. The eighth poem, in contrast, is like an
escape of breath, a withdrawal, an evacuation. It is like a release of pressure,
the mouth of a balloon untied and the air going out of it. Hill seems to

have contrived the poem as an emergency exit from the torment, allowing for a touch of that "vital relaxation" which is the pride of Larkin's poetry. Who is "we"? Who is "they"? Is there any specifiable referent of "Each distant sphere of harmony" or for "such eternity"? The lines seem so ungraspable that one wouldn't feel it if they were being pulled away from him. It seems touched with a light or hollow heart, as if one were to chuckle mindlessly at Hill's finishing the sequence with the phrase, " 'I have not finished'."

No matter how the poem is read, it seems clear that evasiveness must be a crucial part of it. The evasiveness, however, is clearly judged to be just that within the poem. In consequence, by folding the poem back into relation with the rest of the sequence, one discovers that, even though evasive, the poem has a strength and significance equal to its concluding position.

Like the rest of the sequence, this eighth poem is two poems. In one poem, the "we" is the soldier-poets; in the other, the "we" is the modern poet-historian and his like. If the "we" is the soldier-poets, the "they" refers to modern poet-historians who set their subjects apart in an unending line of historical reconstructions of their lives. If, in contrast, the "we" is the modern poet-historian and his like, then the "they" is soldier-poets, whose past lives, dualistically split between the brutish and the spiritually evasive, have determined that the "we" must live, appear, and bear witness as it does. Hill encourages one to slip about with both of these readings by making "Set apart" modify ambiguously both "us" and "they." There is, moreover, an evasiveness about both poems which prevents their being dramatically at odds. At least in the first sentence, which covers the opening seven-and-a-half lines, the "we" seems to refer not just to the soldier-poets and not just to the modern poet-historian and his like, but to all men, indiscriminately. That "we must appear," as "Contractual ghosts of pity," echoes the first line of the entire sequence, suggesting that in "this worldly place," not one's being or reality is in question, but only one's appearance. As by contract, all men, who are really souls, are required to appear pitiably, in the flesh, as in chains. The "they" would then refer vaguely to non-human forces, to the gods of Olympus or the inexorable forces of nature, or, in any case, to whatever is, unspecifiably, "beyond us,/ Each distant sphere of harmony forever/ Poised, unanswerable." Those "spheres" cannot be pressed into definite meaning, because, however one takes them, they slip away as "beyond us" toward the unthinkably non-human. The effect of the first sentence is thus an evaporating away from the fearful definiteness of the end of the seventh poem. Each specific "we" is not just itself to the exclusion of the other, but also the vague, inauthentic, rhetorical "we" whose inflatedness dominated the fifth poem.

The second and third sentences of the poem pull divisively away from this doubling, tripling "we" of the first sentence and also from each other. With its "vaunt and suffer" and its stern resignation, the second sentence clearly belongs to the exemplary self-judging soldier-poets of poems six and seven. In contrast, the third and concluding sentence,

> Then tell me, love,
> How that should comfort us—or anyone
> Dragged half-unnerved out of this worldly place,
> Crying to the end 'I have not finished'.

belongs to the poet-historian, most particularly in the personal, isolate form he takes in the fourth poem, defending his soul against Averroes. As he is heard here, squirming evasively, fudging, self-deceiving, soft, and craven, one feels that Hill is bringing the whole sequence to bear upon himself in the form of a self-judgment as pitiless as that which the soldier-poet of the seventh poem made of himself. The language suggests that the speaker is adopting an unearned conviction (not unlike Milton's conviction in "How soon hath time") that there are superhuman creatures, perhaps seraphim, to do the dragging, that if this world is "this worldly place," then perhaps there is also an otherworldly place, and that, if one is only "half-unnerved," it is because the other half of him senses that his cry, 'I have not finished,' will be heard by him who has otherworldly tasks in store for him. The tone of this last sentence calls attention to itself as self-judged, especially because of the strength of the sentence just before it, where the very idea of "comfort" is unthinkable, and also in contrast with the calm, unruffled objectivity of the poet-historian at the end of the seventh poem, where his descriptive lines judge implicitly not himself, but another.

The most striking way, however, in which Hill brings to the forefront the self-condemnatory quality of this last sentence is in its echoing the end of "Dover Beach." "Then tell me, love" echoes

> Ah, love, let us be true
> To one another! for the world, which seems
> To lie before us like a land of dreams,
> So various, so beautiful, so new,
> Hath really neither joy, nor love, nor light,
> Nor certitude, nor peace, nor help for pain;
> And we are here as on a darkling plain
> Swept with confused alarms of struggle and flight,
> Where ignorant armies clash by night.

The innermost problem of "Dover Beach" is much like that of "Funeral Music": when "the Sea of Faith" has withdrawn "down the vast edges drear/ And naked shingles of the world," and yet armies continue to "clash by night," then they must be called "ignorant" because of the meaninglessness, the bestiality, of their behavior. What else can one do himself but withdraw in fearful comfort with his love, who materializes out of nowhere upon call, her presence unfelt and unprepared for until this last moment. Hill's phrase, "Then tell me, love" brings Arnold's poem to mind with a jolt not because the words or phrasing or even the subject are so much alike, but mainly because his "love" is so unexpected, and Arnold's poem is the classic case of such an arbitrary gesture of evasion. Hill's "love" has none, of course, of the romantic feeling of Arnold's; there is no "ah", no "let us be true." No, his "love" is a gutted word, it is the "love" spoken by shopkeeper to customer. Hill's commonness and softness as poet-historian is exposed, thus, by being pushed up against the commonness and softness of Arnold.

Unquestionably, Hill is crushed by the end of the sequence. But his being so comes through as extraordinary strength, comparable to that of the soldier-poets of poems six and seven. They expose and judge and accept themselves as abandoned. Finding such austere resignation unbearable, Hill makes his evasions, but exposing them and condemning them for what they are. He shares the need of Eliot to align himself as poet-historian with a superior position like that of the martyr-saint, but, unlike Eliot, at the very time he gives vent to that need, Hill exposes it to the withering light of truth. Against Eliot's tendency, even in *Four Quartets*, to withdraw into "a world of speculation," Hill binds the meditativeness of his poetry fiercely to ethical action in a worldly sense. Because of this, it must be sharply distinguished from that philosophical aspect of Eliot's poetry which has led Alessandro Serpieri, in his *T. S. Eliot: le strutture profonde* (Bologna, 1973), to treat Eliot as a precursor of all the main "deep structure" movements of the century, which begin close to experience, close to poetry, close to the pang of the flesh of language, but then light-headedly beat a quick retreat to the mountainous clouds of abstractive vacuousness. Hill himself underwent the movement, but did not succumb to the massiveness of its inertial drag. Instead he has wrestled himself away from it and bent himself back into a strange, dramatic oneness with men, both of the past, like Tiptoft, Rivers, and Suffolk, and the present, like T. S. Eliot, who are fundamentally different from him.

CALVIN BEDIENT

On Geoffrey Hill

The quickly building consensus that
Geoffrey Hill is 'the best poet now writing in England' means less than it
might in view both of his troubled competition (but poets are not really
in a position to compete) and of his own profoundly troubled talent.

As for the 'competition' it is true that, a few years ago, when one
brought to mind Charles Tomlinson, W. S. Graham, C. H. Sisson, Philip
Larkin, R. S. Thomas, Donald Davie, Ted Hughes, Basil Bunting and
Stevie Smith, never mind Hill, one wondered when there had last been
in England a group so abundantly and variously gifted. But one missed in
this group a figure around whom the others would fall into place: an ex-
clamation point of the age, a commanding sensibility.

One knew that Larkin, with his arresting but accidental lack of
animal faith, was not central: that Hughes, with his gothic glorifications
of the same faith, was no less eccentric. Even Tomlinson seemed brook-
bottom remote. For life as an unpredictable manifold, even more for a
manifold response to life, one had to turn to Donald Davie, despite his
pinched Puritan severity, and to deliberately dotty and doughty Stevie
Smith. But their thinnish manner left one hungry for a grand merger of
sound, diction, feeling, thought—for a manner generous despite disap-
proval, doubt, irony.

Yes, it was less a moral failing than a failure of generous response
to experience that one noted in these poets. And this latter failure kept
back something from the language. Though Larkin charged his lines with
eloquence in certain moments of regret, though Hughes wrote plangently

From *Critical Quarterly* 2, vol. 23 (Summer 1981). Copyright © 1981 by Manchester
University Press.

in *Lupercal*, though Graham foxed English delightfully, still a pall lay on the language of the time.

Thomas Kinsella got at the cause in his essay 'The divided mind':

It was no news that the human mind was an abyss, and that the will, just as much as the imagination, was capable of every evil. But it was something new that creatures out of Hieronymous Bosch should have materialized in the world . . .; it is something new to have had the orderly but insane holocausts imagined by Leonardo da Vinci set loose on the earth in an act of logical but monstrous choice. The coming to reality of these apparently fantastic images is an inner catastrophe; we have opened up another area of ourselves and found something new that horrifies, but that even more intensely *disappoints*. The realization of this disappointment seems to me the most significant thing in contemporary poetry: it is the source of that feeling of precariousness which is to be found in the best poets now living.

This precariousness, or scepticism of the good, the elevated, the communal, has made English nervous and self-conscious.

One way around disappointment, whatever its risks of shallowness, is the gift of a healthy nature. Seamus Heaney has it, and thus far avoiding complacency (though not a would-be-awed pose in his bog poems) and distinguished by a Hopkins- and Lowell-trained ear for packed lines, he has become a source of increasing interest, pleasure, and hope.

Another solution—more difficult and more significant—is to be fierce with precariousness, in both senses of the phrase. Kinsella himself has attempted this—with precarious results. Geoffrey Hill too has been savaged by 'the realization of . . . disappointment' and has been savage about it. His early poetry is sick with it, stymied. In *Mercian Hymns* he fared better, roused like a cornered animal despite his trembling. The volume has the scary control and exhilaration of Marlowe on the trail of Kurtz. Hill's moral rage magnanimously allowed human and natural life a barbarous glamour; his language prickled not only with irony but with ambivalence, a begrudging excitement. Then in the best parts of *Tenebrae* he tried a different tact, not unsuccessful—a disarming tolerance Christ-touched but also like that of time, time that survives its every mistake.

King Log (1968) and even more *For the Unfallen* (1959) now look like apprentice work spangled by greatness. To take to disappointment as to a cross is to court excess, and the early volumes show as much weakness as strength, as much sickness as health—as well as a good deal of derivativeness.

In the self-torturing state Hill was in then he could write brilliantly but not well. If a poet is only so good as his relation to his material Hill neglected his even as in one sense he made too much of it—he wanted history to confess the worst, the courtroom of conscience to cry 'Atrocity!' But really it was himself he had on trial; he was secretly self-absorbed. He could not get the tone right because he wanted to excoriate himself for being human, if not for being Hill; he was not humane to himself and tone, the crux of every poem, is the humane aspect of language.

For Hill, history effectively ended with the aftermath of the Second World War, the catastrophe of his own young postwar conscience. Always he writes back from there, his sensibility spreading back like a stain. (Where Larkin is chockful of contemporary England, Hill might never have left his wartime wireless.) Hill illustrates—tending as he does toward the exemplary—what Stephen Spender called the European position, that 'to be alive is to be an outpost' of the past.

Yet Hill was relating history less than inventing nightmares, and it showed in his febrile language, self-conscious silences, lurching ironies. The poems argued a staggering need to be blinded in 'renunciation's glare'. Moral sorrow lodged in Hill's breast like an arrow it would be death to remove. His humaneness harrowed him and *that* was what one noticed. His own guilt upstaged history's. He postured: 'I believe in my/Abandonment . . .' Again (also from 'Funeral music'); '. . . blindly we lie down, blindly/Among carnage the most delicate souls/Tup in their marriage-blood, gasping "Jesus" '. A rage to share in atrocity as if it were the last real community on earth.

Sicklied o'er with guilt, all too decent, Hill was incapacitated to write about brutal power with the fearless simplicity (witness Nazim Hikmet or Yannis Ritsos) that goes straight like a stake for the Cyclops' eye. He bit his own tongue, was too tragic-gestured. His compassion lacked warmth and directness. The two 'formal' elegies 'for the Jews in Europe' proved all too formal-bookish. They minced with obscurity, with overplayed fastidiousness. Nor was his despair clear and universal, like Beckett's. It retained something murky, private.

Not to look at evil directly is to let it bloat with myth. 'I am circumspect', Hill says in the second of 'Three Baroque meditations', 'Lifting the spicy lid of my tact/To sniff at the myrrh. It is perfect/In its impalpable bitterness,/Scent of a further country whose worse/Furies promenade and bask their claws'. This 'further country' is the fetor of conscience: simple fantasy. Though aware that it's gothic stuff Hill lets it 'promenade' anyway. He seems to enjoy being mired in such falseness. Grounds for self-divorce.

To sniff 'tactfully' at evil is to create a sensational interest in it, leading to a still more would-be-immaculate reaction. Thus 'Funeral Music', the major sequence before *Mercian Hymns,* alternately cries havoc (though not the 'grunts' and 'Shrieks' Hill naively said he wanted) and offers sugared rhetoric to conscience. Space does not allow me to trace the frequent shifts from poem to poem, but consider something so apparently venial as the fatal slight falseness of tone in the sweet sixth poem:

> My little son, when you could command marvels
> Without mercy, outstare the wearisome
> Dragon of sleep, I rejoiced above all—
> A stranger well-received in your kingdom.
> On those pristine fields I saw humankind
> As it was named by the Father; fabulous
> Beasts rearing in stillness to be blessed . . .

This is a mere dream of a dream, downy with sentiment, a stern moralist's holiday in the land of innocence. Or take the solemn pep-rhetoric of the final poem: 'If it is without/Consequence when we vaunt and suffer . . .' If it is, Tennysonian horror; so it must not be. God may have absconded but exists. 'What I dare not is a waste history/Or void rule.'

But as notable in the early volumes as the shadow-shows of guilt was a monstrous gift of expression. To be so sly of conscience is to be able to turn words queasy, discover soft places in them, make them burn; to be so anguished is to want an answering sonority. Hill's great if perfidious intelligence, his brilliantly unforgiving sensibility, was matched by an ear schooled in grand styles.

In his second volume he began to enter the twentieth century, to cease being orotund. 'Undesirable you may have been, untouchable/you were not'; 'Recall the wind's/Flurrying, darkness over the human mire'— the pitch here is human and pitches directly into life. He could make the meter whip-ripple, the end loom up fast: 'Gargantuan mercies whetted by a scent/Of mortal sweat.' The dynamics could be exactly right—*piano* but you could hear them in a storm.

What Hill had yet to gain was enough distance from his material (or himself) to be direct and just through an entire poem. In *Mercian Hymns* he was able to accomplish precisely that, and for an entire volume.

Here, though moral irony holds court, matters more nearly speak for themselves. The work lacks horror-mongering—myrrh-sniffing, even. Although little of the little actually known about King Offa is used, the biographical idea of the work straitens it. Offa, part of Hill's childhood, is not overbad—he's just human, just bad. Human nature in its pride, caprice, treachery, guilt, Offa is brought onto the page in a tone that avoids both mercy and excess, a tone we cannot get around.

Poet and protagonist circle one another in mutual need and distrust. Offa needs Hill ('Exile or pilgrim') to set him 'once more upon that ground: my rich and desolate childhood'. The poet obliges, for, a Narcissus looking dizzily into the horror-pool of time, his own nature, is it not Offa that he would drown in?

He is saved by his irony—his askesis in the sensuality of time. Poet and king are close as conspirators, as ego and alter ego, crime and conscience—but Hill's irony, the thin end of a blade that never fully reveals itself, cuts him off from history, placing him at the juncture of Christian judgement.

Yet the end of the work is not judgement. This is its revolutionary change from the earlier books. Balanced between condemnation and celebration, it evades eschatological ideology, just as it evades the Modernist ideology of despair.

The characteristics of this last were drawn by Georg Lukács as follows: (1) 'Man . . . is by nature solitary, asocial . . .'; (2) 'The individual, retreating into himself in despair at the cruelty of the age, may experience an intoxicated fascination with his forlorn condition'; (3) 'The denial of history, of development and thus of perspective becomes the mark of true insight into the nature of reality.'

Like a nearly total eclipse, this ideology is present in the *Hymns*. Offa and Hill meet intimately across eight centuries as if no one else had any claim on them—isolates of the despair that anyone else matters, that history is anything but a pit. Their shared solitariness is centuries deep. Offa, 'the presiding genius of the West Midlands', is the agent as Hill is the poet of history, both ubiquitous insiders, predatory dreamers; at large. 'Threatened by phone-calls at midnight, venomous letters', Offa is at once the 'cruelty of the age' and the forlorn individual in retreat.

The lowering skies of these hymns is not split by revelation. The women may work tapestries 'riddled by mysteries' but the men trudge 'out of the dark, scraping their boots free from lime-splodges and phlegm.' Salvation is a rumour—while, from the back of history, the corpse of Cernunnos pitches 'dayward its feral horns'. 'Coagulations of frogs' in 'marlpools that lay unstirring'—inert congestion—is the rule. The catharsis: violence. The historical sense fastens on to batterings as if onto hope itself, the hope, anyway, of a clearing-out. Then, from the appalled stillness and silence, sidles away.

But not only Hill's moral antagonisms, his vital powers abjure despair. No matter that 'denial of history' seems implicit in the peculiarly disjointed structure, the anachronisms and the rejection of narrative. No matter, even, that the poem ends by annihilating the mythical imagination ('. . . he entered into the last dream of Offa the King'), an imagination that had already borne nothing-ward the paralyzed historical sense. The work none the less rests in confidence in its own construction, confidence in language, eloquence, arresting beauty, intimated splendor—in these as much as in tell-tale irony. Exquisitely crafted, with never a word too many or few, a word not mesmerizingly right, it is its own best testimony to the human power to manage recalcitrant material—a concern introduced at the juridical level by the epigraph from the Christian monarchist C. H. Sisson.

Hill's imagination enjoys what his judgment deplores. It creates the reality that justice must confront. And it thus does justice to worldly energies. As truculently splendid as they are ferociously economical, the hymns get at things—'bellow of whale-bone and dung', 'peppermint and confetti'—with honest relish. Hill's imagination is brought over at last to the concreteness, more the atavism to which dreams are faithful. Happy for us that he writes about his own backyard, backward-reaching midlands: his imagination, fleeing conscience like Daphne from Apollo, sprouts roots from its toes, twigs from its fingers. Everything in the work is aesthetically vigorous, self-justified. We find awe of nature's remoteness, mystery, savagery; awe of the same things in Offa, ourselves writ large. We find 'epiphanies, vertebrae of the chimera, armour of wild bee's larvae': the imagination paying tribute to itself. We see why the poems are called 'hymns'.

Offa and Hill, wildness and irony, end in a stand-off. The work has the truth and energy of conflict. The style reflects the complication, is sensuous and severe at once. The 'prose' I take to be earnest ballast drawing Hill down to actuality; the nonetheless paced, sonorous writing as his intention to celebrate it; and the wrought economy his refusal to be intoxicated by it (the more so as it is confused by dreams).

The language is dignified while trying to be what it says: both self and other, judgment and participation. First the measure then the slipperily repetitious sounds of 'The lamps grew plump with oily reliable light' form instances. The language catches itself with the bitten apple in hand.

One would say Latinisms are Hill's distinction if his Anglo-Saxon did not grip so. 'They brewed and pissed amid splendour; their latrine seethed its estuary through nettles. They are scattered to your collations, moldywarp'—the one, the other, the one, the other, like the black and white on a pasturing bull. Tradition and originality, familiar cadence and furbishing word, merge no less successfully: 'After that shadowy, thrashing midsummer hailstorm, Earth lay for a while, the ghost-bride of livid Thor, butcher of strawberries.' Adventurously beautiful, forceful is 'ghost-bride', 'livid Thor', 'butcher of strawberries'; hardly less elegant their continuity with the best use of English before.

By fending off neither the mind nor the senses, Hill opens his language to everything. To moral nuance in physical description: 'In dawn-light the troughed water floated a damson bloom of dust' (from a hymn on a nail factory, where neither beauty nor tragedy steps back for the other but together draw out a torn, uncompromised response). To drama, inter-nalising pop-ups: 'Where best to stand? Easter sunrays catch the oblique face of Adam scrumping through leaves . . .' To surprises of voice: 'Tell everything to Mother, darling, and God bless.' To wit; rapture; rue. He creates a poetry at once crisp, sensual, and grand.

Everything in the hymns argues strength. Above all its refusal to smother things by wrapping them up. For the individual really is solitary, and not; time deniable, and not; the past a father—demonic, pathetic—who perhaps should, and perhaps cannot, be exorcised. A choice would be ideological. Art challenges ideology.

A work of rare inspiration, *Mercian Hymns* provided what was long overdue: a modern English poetic masterpiece of real magnitude (and at the same time, with the qualifications noted, a modernist masterpiece, disturbingly complex, tauntingly disjunctive). No surprise that Hill's sub-sequent volume proved a lesser achievement—but *Tenebrae* is disappoint-ing, none the less. Reflecting a failure of nerve, it reacts against the strengths of *Mercian Hymns*. Structure is rounded up, style strapped, conscience sent to church, if only to other people's churches. And history, that cauldron of the hymns, is here a cold pot. If *Mercian Hymns* is the crime, *Tenebrae* is the penitence.

In the three devotional sequences Hill packs in his formidable powers and docilely copies sixteenth-century Spanish *a lo divino* lyrics ('Pentecost Castle'), sonnets by Lope de Vega and Quevedo ('Lachrimae'), and T. S. Eliot's type of variable long poem ('Tenebrae'). The writing is all ceremony and poorly lit, tenebrae indeed. What is Hill screening behind these im-itations? What is the actual status of his faith?

The devotional sequences are cop-outs, dismaying to anyone who wants Hill to write at his best—to be honest. 'I went out early / To the far field / ermine and lily / and yet a child / Love stood before me / in that place / prayers could not lure me / To Christ's house': this has the ersatz charm of an antique reproduction. It mews—one cannot be a sixteenth-century Spanish poet today, in so artificial a mode, and still have all one's wits about one. The sonnets are still more mawkish:

> Crucified Lord, you swim upon your cross
> and never move. Sometimes in dreams of hell
> the body moves to no avail
> and is at one with that eternal loss.
>
> You are the castaway of drowned remorse,
> you are the world's atonement on the hill.
> This is your body twisted by our skill
> into a patience proper for redress . . .

Lackadaisical, sentimental, pompous. 'To no avail', 'that eternal loss', 'the castaway of drowned remorse', 'the world's atonement on the hill', 'proper for redress'—the writing is a curiously bored impersonation of devotion. Or take the title poem: 'This is the ash-pit of the lily-fire, / this is the questioning at the long tables, / this is . . .'—this is T. S. Eliot. 'The best societies of hell / acknowledge this, aroused by what they know' is simply bombast. 'O light of light, supreme delight'—you long to say it is all in fun.

Perhaps Hill is after all too proud and feral for the posture of penitence. It speaks to and of only a certain crushed part of him. So in his kneelings he mimics others, to get it 'right'. But the beanstalk was for Jack, not the giant, whose mistake lay in trying to go down.

That Hill is in retreat not only from his own powers but once again from worldly power in general—'Anything', he wrote in his early poem 'Solomon's mines', 'to get up and go / (let the hewn gates clash to) / Without looking round / Out of that strong land'—is apparent in his fine historical sequence, 'An apology for the revival of Christian architecture in England'. Its thirteen sonnets unite in the theme of an England whose historical fires are so banked that it is ready for a religious revival: the other life. With its sweet trembling hope the theme almost goes underground in embarrassment and the oblique title is more wince than wink.

A brief outline may help. Sonnet 1: 'Religion of the heart . . . again / rejoices in old hymns of servitude': Christianity subdues the Western heresy of romance. Sonnet 2: Damon laments Clorinda in sunless Yorkshire, 1654; the air grows 'cold / in the region of mirrors', the limbo between 'Religion of the heart' and proper devotional servitude. Sonnet 3: Religion of the heart proves headstrong, devastating, bitter. Sonnets 4, 5, and 6: British India's expense of spirit, 'sated upon the stillness of the bride': Imperialism seduced by the romance of India. Sonnet 7: 'Platonic England', spent, 'grasps its tenantry where wild-eyed poppies raddle tawny farms / and wild swans root in lily-clouded lakes', wildness now pastorally decorative. Sonnet 8: an exemplary religious vocation ('reckoning and judicious prayer') in snowberried Platonic England. Sonnet 9: England's Platonic self-survival again, 'replete with complex fortunes that are gone, / beset by dynasties of moods and clouds'. Sonnet 10: 'Theology makes good bedside reading' (a statement only half-ironic). Sonnet 11: England's woodsy Arthurian magnificence replaced by 'the half-built ruins of the new estate'; time to ' "clap your hands" so that the dove takes flight'—for inner removal and renewal. Sonnet 12: a godmother who like Platonic England has survived her carnality, near her a stuffed 'owl immortal in its crystal dome'. Last, sonnet 13: celebration of 'that kingdom' that 'grows / greener in winter, essence of the year', the sun none the less returning to cottaged England:

> In grange and cottage girls rise from their beds
> by candlelight and mend their ruined braids.
> Touched by the cry of the iconoclast,
> how the rose-window blossoms with the sun!

Vitality, time, change—these threaten to cease altogether in this new churchyard perspective, where only winter 'grows / greener'. Time gives way like a false floor: 'The pigeon purrs in the wood; the wood has gone'; is played out: 'and wiry heath-fern scatters its fresh rust'. What was endorsed to avoid a 'void rule' has begun to make a void of what is ruled.

Ever so gently the new tone draws the blood of things:

> The twittering pipistrelle, so strange and close,
> plucks its curt flight through the moist eventide;
> the children thread among old avenues
> of snowberries, clear-calling as they fade.

The tenderness is like amber—it preserves, kills. A certain diffuseness of aim, implicit in elegy if not eulogy, afflicts these mild sonnets, which are anyway biding time till the Second Coming. (Even the most dramatic one, 'Who are these coming to the Sacrifice?', ends in a waiting-room atmosphere.) As sonnets the poems are not activated: one reads them like tombstones. Little happens in them, little through them. Platonic England, Platonic sonnets.

Yet one or two short poems aside, the sequence contains Hill's best writing next to *Mercian Hymns*. Whatever his eschatological bias the poet does not confuse himself with his material. And tenderness, even tolerance acknowledges the world's body, giving substance to the line.

Then too, if narrative hardly takes root where the end has already been decreed, still the poet borrows its devices. Before its chilling de-nouement, for instance, 'A Short history of British India (II)' presents this 98.6°, internal view:

> Our law-books overrule the emperors.
> The mango is the bride-bed of light. Spring
> jostles the flame-tree. But new mandates bring
> new images of faith, good subahdars!

Here Hill enters the British and Indian minds almost simultaneously, with impartiality and fish-quick, fish-still intuitiveness. In 'Who are these coming to the Sacrifice?' the initial paratactic impressions rest on the story that follows ('. . . the hired chaise / tore through the fir-grove, scattered kinsmen flung / buckshot and bridle . . .') like a florid, leisurely capital on a column. Throughout, the resistance of lived life is posed against a mournful drift and tone. The whole sequence ends tensely in a triple rising, triple touching, and triple mending (those of the girls in grange and cottage, the iconoclast, and the sun).

The pentameter, every pause and syllable of it, is earned. Hill may do nothing notably new with the line but he makes a crowning use of it. Though even English poets have favoured shorter lines these last two dec-ades, tradition can still be wonderfully high-piled in good pentameter, the audience for it still predisposed to be moved. Hill gives it a remote-hearted perfection. His temperament homes to its circumspect formality. Ten un-hurried syllables tap out authority, caution, measure. With him the line has the height of a judge's bench, practised patience.

Perhaps *Mercian Hymns*, haunted by pentameter though it is, freed Hill from fear of the line. In any case he shows a new ease with it, having mastered (without silencing) its almost inevitable echoes. Consider a poem not in a sequence, 'Terribilis est Locus Iste: Gauguin and the Pont-Aven School:

> Briefly they are amazed. The marigold-fields
> mell and shudder and the travellers,
> in sudden exile burdened with remote
> hieratic gestures, journey to no end
> beyond the vivid severance of each day,
> strangeness at doors, a different solitude
> between the mirror and the window, marked
> visible absences . . .

The sentence winds on, at once luxurious and on-edge, through yet another quatrain, all but lost in the irreality of a life without seraphic and stormy depths. How resourceful this poet is with pentameter. He can make it a mouthful and eyeful: 'by silvery vistas frothed with convolvulus'; rake in with it as magisterially as time: 'Primroses; salutations; the miry skull / Of a half-eaten ram; viscous wounds in earth opening. What seraphs are afoot . . .'; take a lithe Augustan turn: 'While friends defected, you stayed and were sure, / fervent in reason, watchful of each name'; poise it so that it seems unmoveable: 'warheads of mushrooms round the filter-pond'; fetch it touchingly short of breath: 'and the lost delicate suitors who could sing.'

If Hill's conquest of pentameter is post-Oedipal, his retreat from history and passion and from original structures suggests precisely an Oedipal crisis. The horrifying and disappointing father, contested and even bested in the hymns, his fate sealed by that 'last dream', is now triumphed over merely—and sadly—in being pronounced deceased:

> . . . goldgrimy shafts and pillars of the sun.
>
> Weightless magnificence upholds the past.
> Cement recesses smell of fur and bone
> and berries wrinkle in the badger-run . . .

(or nearly deceased: there are still 'warheads of mushrooms round the filter-pond'). The wintry, asexual Son is accordingly uplifted, causing only the rose-window to blossom, while waking girls mend their ruined braids.

In *King Log* Hill reeled from carnality; in *Mercian Hymns*, teased it like a boy prodding a scorpion with a stick; in *Tenebrae*, interred it. Is the drama over?

With the qualified exception of *Mercian Hymns*, has it not all been like a dream? Kinsella's analysis of the contemporary poet insures and justifies disappointment—but in fact it remains to be justified with each poem. Hill's (like Kinsella's) has usually been beforehand. It has led the poet by the nose.

Perhaps his greatest liability is one other poets might envy: fear of his own powers. All the more remarkable then that he wrote *Mercian Hymns*. He thus illuminated a bold and difficult excellence, creating a standard of truth and structural genius to which we may feel disposed to hold him. Conspicuous elevation, evidence of upheaval, ups and downs—in this case there is something in a name.

A. K. WEATHERHEAD

Hunter of Forms

The impetus for a poem by Geoffrey Hill is metaphoric. He *realizes*, he says, not in situations or themes but in terms of metaphors. The metaphor is the starting point; the poet must find its true context, the poem, by conscious intellection. His poetry is difficult, and for the awestruck and embarrassed reviewer, most certain of its merit and most uncertain of its meaning, the dictum of T. S. Eliot that poetry may communicate before it is understood has come conveniently to hand. In an age in which much poetry moves toward openness, this is closed. Although many contemporary poets call for the creative contribution of their readers, Hill controls his in that complementary exercise; Hill would not speak as Harwood does of readers establishing *individual* readings for themselves, creating, in effect, a number of different poems. More than many of his contemporaries, Hill knows how he wants to be read. And while many contemporary poets deliberately avoid depth, behind a single word in Hill, there may be an ocean. The word is not the correlative of an act, as in some recent poetry, nor replete with primal energy; it is packed with meaning. It is not coincidence that of all its predecessors, Hill's poetry recalls most acutely the somber music of Allen Tate, who was aware early of the new trends but whose late work, even, is strictly of the older tradition.

A poem of Hill's may exist in relationships between elements that are neither logically connected nor necessarily to be received chronologically. He favors, for example, the sequence (like Matthew Mead but not for precisely the same reasons), in which, while the sequential nature of the arrangement is not remarkable, the meaning of one poem is colored

From *The British Dissonance: Essays on Ten Contemporary Poets.* Copyright © 1983 by the Curators of the University of Missouri. University of Missouri Press.

by its reaction against others. He uses titles, subtitles, and sometimes even dedications and epigraphs to qualify various parts of a poem, and that poem may be said to comment upon these elements. The last poem of a sequence titled "Of Commerce and Society" (a title that comes from Allen Tate's "More Sonnets at Christmas, 1942," quoted in the eipgraph to Hill's series) is preceded by passages that create a kind of field: the poem's title, a dedication, and an epigraph. If we are to perceive all its irony, we must read the poem with all these elements in mind, along with the title of the whole sequence:

> VI *The Martyrdom of Saint Sebastian*
> Homage to Henry James
> *'But then face to face.'*

The poem then begins:

> Naked, as if for swimming, the martyr
> Catches his death in a little flutter
> Of plain arrows. A grotesque situation,
> But priceless, and harmless to the nation.
>
> Consider such pains 'crystalline': then fine art
> Persists where most crystals accumulate.
> History can be scraped clean of its old price.

The martyrdom of the saint, popularly thought to have been effected by archery and made the subject of Renaissance paintings, is travestied in the first two lines, "Naked, as if for swimming" and "Catches his death," the common idiom for getting a cold. By cleaning the picture, "History can be scraped clean of its old price," that is, of sin and the commerce in the general title; "priceless" is also related to commerce, though colloquially it suggests "funny"; "a little flutter," referring immediately to arrows, can also have the commercial meaning of an adventure either on the stock market or at the race track. "Crystalline" and "fine art" one may associate with Henry James. The cleaning process relates ironically to spiritual transformation, seeing not as through a glass darkly but face to face, the expectation of St. Paul, who is quoted in the epigraph.

The poem is an extreme example of Hill's practice of spreading out points of reference between the parts of a poem and its context, a practice sufficiently characteristic to warrant notice of another instance. The body of the poem "Ovid in the Third Reich" from Hill's second volume, *King Log* (also collected in *Somewhere Is Such a Kingdom*), reacts against the two elements in the title and an epigraph from the *Amores* in which Ovid declares that any woman is innocent unless she confess her guilt. The poem opens,

> I love my work and my children. God
> Is distant, difficult. Things happen.

The reference to the Third Reich in the title and the spurious innocence recommended by Ovid in the eipgraph serve to draw out of these apparently innocent, inert lines the terrible history of the concentration camps.

The elements within a poem itself, themselves often obscure, may be related by links similar to those that connect epigraphs and titles rather than by an explicitly logical progression. Hill's practice of issuing points of reference that react against each other is not incompatible with the idea of the poem as music, a medium that naturally transcends its necessary temporality. We designate literature as musical when there are remarkable melodic effects of vowels or consonants (as in Tennyson, "mouthing out his hollow oes and aes," or in "Brag, sweet tenor bull," in Basil Bunting's *Briggflatts*), or, more significantly, when the literary structure is based on specific musical models (as in Strindberg's *Ghost Sonata*, for example, and Eliot's *Four Quartets*). We also refer to literature as music when we don't quite know what else to say about it—an alternative to Eliot's dictum about understanding and communication.

In an essay, "Funeral Music," Hill says about the sequence of the same title that he was "attempting a florid grim music broken by grunts and shrieks." There are, to be sure, melodic passages in the sequence, "Fire / Flares in the pit, ghosting upon stone," and resounding clashes of vowel and consonant,

>   we are dying
>   To satisfy fat Caritas, those
>   Wiped jaws of stone.

Perhaps it is rather a choreography of motifs and images, related to a theme and free of logical advance, that Hill's comment invites us to notice. The sonnets dwell on the human condition, its solipsism, the fallen flesh to which the aspiring soul is ineluctably wed, the pain of earthly existence and its inconsequence in the soul's history—an awful Manichean vision. The main theme, the conception of this world as "restless / Habitation, no man's dwelling-place" and life as a lingering pain, is set in the first poem:

>   Processionals in the exemplary cave,
>   Benediction of shadows. Pomfret. London.

> The voice fragrant with mannered humility,
> With an equable contempt for this World,
> 'In honorem Trinitatis'. Crash. The head
> Struck down into a meaty conduit of blood.

Much that follows in the sequence is here anticipated. "The exemplary cave" is Plato's cave of shadows, and the conception described by that allegory fits the pervading theme of *contemptus mundi*. The moving figures that make the shadows on the stone wall in the fable are by extension the historical figures in the procession that moves through the sequence, "Creatures of such rampant state," as they are later portrayed. Pomfret was the scene of the putative murder of Richard II, which preceded the civil strife of the Wars of the Roses (the second sonnet begins, "For whom do we scrape our tribute of pain— / For none but the ritual king?," reminding us of *2 Henry IV* in which the Archbishop turns insurrection to religion "with the blood / Of fair King Richard, scraped from Pomfret stones"), the castle being adjacent to the site of the Battle of Towton, one of the major battles of those wars, which appears here in the sequence. London was the stage for the beheading of John Tiptoft, Earl of Worcester, to whom the sequence is dedicated, along with the Duke of Suffolk and the Earl Rivers, all of whom suffered beheading during the second half of the fifteenth century— three lords, powerful men, lovers of the arts, whose fortunes once high had revolved on the wheel. The voice and what it says belong, as the essay informs, to Tiptoft, who commanded "that he should be decapitated in three strokes 'in honor of the Trinity.' " The fate of his head, unmitigated by his piety, contributes to the theme running throughout—the grievous lot of humankind on this earth, the "stark ground of this pain."

References to the Wars of the Roses swirl about the central Manichean theme and provide a smoky glamour. Other motifs reflect each other throughout in idea or image clusters: fire and stone are associated, torches and atonement, armies and flashing light, blindness and reconciliation, trumpets and purification, silence and innocence.

A second theme in "Funeral Music" is the duty of the poet in relation to the demands of the dead to be reported aright in the world. The poem's function is to cleanse the past, to liberate history from the stain occasioned by its association with putrescent flesh and sin. The motif has already been glimpsed in "The Martyrdom of Saint Sebastian"; we see it again when, for example, "The lily rears its gouged face / From the provided loam." The poem's act is one of love; as death frees the soul from its earthly bondage, so the word may free history from the tainted mire of human veins—hence the relationship between the instrument of death and the angel that brings the word, as the three lords "dispose themselves to receive each / Pentecostal blow from axe or seraph." The theme of poetry as an act of cleansing is announced in the second sonnet,

> For whom do we scrape our tribute of pain—
> For none but the ritual king? We meditate
> A rueful mystery; we are dying
> To satisfy fat Caritas

(the "tribute of pain" and "dying" must surely be taken to refer to the creative act, to the making of poetry), and reflected throughout the sequence: "trampled / Acres" are "blanched by sleet"; darkness falls over the human mire; a vision of life controlled by intellect shows "an unpeopled region / Of ever new-fallen snow." Beyond the sonnet sequence, also, Hill's work is pervaded by the craving for purity, for the antisepsis of the mind as opposed to the corruption of the body, and for the cleansing of the past so that it may reappear as in childhood's innocent kingdom, purified by time and returning into the present as a part of a harmony. The sixth sonnet of "Funeral Music," for example, looks back through a child's vision to idealized images of men.

> My little son, when you could command marvels
> Without mercy, outstare the wearisome
> Dragon of sleep, I rejoiced above all—
> A stranger well-received in your kingdom.
> On those pristine fields I saw humankind
> As it was named by the Father; fabulous
> Beasts rearing in stillness to be blessed.

Although the poet has this duty of love to perform, poetry is nevertheless an act performed in pain or even disgust. It is occasionally associated with claws, as in "Words clawed my mind as though they had smelt / Revelation's flesh." And ease is reprehensible; the first part of "Annunciations," again, from *Somewhere Is Such a Kingdom*, closes in contempt of the trencher fury of respectable poetasters:

> all who attend to fiddle or to harp
> For betterment, flavour their decent mouths
> With gobbets of the sweetest sacrifice.

The second part, on the other hand, closes with lines on the theme of painful creation, the burden of love:

> Choicest beasts
> Suffuse the gutters with their colourful blood.
> Our God scatters corruption. Priests, martyrs,

> Parade to this imperious theme: "O Love
> You know what pains succeed; be vigilant; strive
> To recognize the damned among your friends."

The act of going into the past and bringing history into an innocent childhood kingdom in the present, noted above, produced in 1971 a sequence of prose poems, *Mercian Hymns,* in which the duty to history hardly seems a painful one. The sequence opens:

> King of the perennial holly-groves, the riven sand-
>   stone: overlord of the M5: architect of the his-
>   toric rampart and ditch, the citadel at Tamworth . . .
>   . . . contractor
>   to the desirable new estates: saltmaster: money-
>   changer . . .
> "I liked that," said Offa, "sing it again."

The poems are to be regarded, Hill says, as commentaries on the subjects supplied by the headings. The so-called headings are not set each above its own hymn but are gathered separately in both *Mercian Hymns* and *Somewhere Is Such a Kingdom.* Almost all the headings relate the individual poems to episodes or activities in the life of Offa, eighth-century king of Mercia, to his attributes, or to legacies of his reign. In a few poems, the content does not concern Offa directly: number 14, headed "Offa's Laws," presents the persona of a West Midland rural magistrate; number 25, "Opus Anglicanum," is a lament for one of the old nailers of Bromsgrove, a town in the English Midlands. The headings are not rubrics but elements in juxtaposition to the parts of the poems proper, after the fashion noted in the earlier volumes. The parts of the poems, generally two, three, or four in number, set off as separate paragraphs, are themselves thus loosely related to each other in many of the poems. Individually, they may be clear and in this respect quite different from the elements in earlier poems; but the connections between them are often obscure, subtle, and tenuous.

Connections may be effected, for instance, by a motif derived from connotations or etymologies or from the fifth dictionary meaning of a word. Poem number 20 is headed "Offa's 'Defence of the English People' " and has only two parts. The first presents the "primeval heathland" with the bones of mice and birds, where "bees made provision, mantling the inner walls of their burh." The second is as follows:

> Coil entrenched England: brickwork and paintwork
>   stalwart above hacked marl. The clashing prim-
>   ary colours—'Ethandune', 'Catraeth', 'Maldon',

'Pengwern'. Steel against yew and privet. Fresh
dynasties of smiths.

The small brick houses and bungalows with clashing colors are only too
familiar on the English scene, but they are, each of them, the Englishman's
home, his castle; without undue exercise of the fancy, they may be thought
of as speaking to an England defended, "entrenched," and now presumably
at peace. They are "stalwart," which comes from the Anglo-Saxon *stath-
olwyrthe*, meaning having firm foundations. A note draws attention to the
popular use in England of the name of ancient battles for suburban houses.
The battles are presumably the foundations upon which England now rests,
so that now the peaceful domestic art of clipping the hedge may supersede
the art of war. But with the association of the battles, "hacked" and "clashing" take on a fighting sense; "smith," here primarily a common English
surname, becomes associated with steel; and "steel," no longer merely the
garden shears, suggests ordnance. Then the battle connotations reach back
to the first part of the poem, where against a background of battle—the
heathland strewn with bones—the bees, like the Englishmen, embellish
the walls of the "burh," etymologically a fortress.

The eleventh poem, "Offa's Coins," has four parts and shows a
similar reticulation formed by underlying meanings and associations of
words. The poem has four parts; the first part and selections from the others
are as follows:

> Coins handsome as Nero's; of good substance and
>   weight. *Offa Rex* resonant in silver, and the
>   names of his moneyers. They struck with account-
>   able tact. They could alter the king's face.
>
> Exactness of design was to deter imitation; mutil-
>   ation if that failed.
>
> Swathed bodies in the long ditch; one eye upstaring.
>   It is safe to presume, here, the king's anger. . . .
>
> Seasons touched and retouch-
> ed the soil.
>
>   Crepitant oak forest where the boar
> furrowed black mould, his snout intimate with
> worms and leaves.

A selection of the connecting links includes those between "struck" and
"anger," "struck" and "mould," altering the face and "mutilation," "tact"
and "touched," "design" and "seasons," "soil" and "mould," and "ditch"

and "furrowed." The association of coins, corpses, and the soil is discussed below.

"The Offa who figures in this sequence," says Hill's note to the whole book, "might perhaps most usefully be regarded as the presiding genius of the West Midlands, his dominion enduring from the middle of the eighth century until the middle of the twentieth (and possibly beyond). The indication of such a timespan will, I trust, explain and to some extent justify a number of anachronisms." Parts of individual poems apparently disparate may in fact be related through the identity of the poet in the three roles he plays throughout: himself, himself in childhood, and Offa the king. In number 29, "The Death of Offa," the penultimate poem of the sequence, the poet as child plays ludo (a game of dice and counters) with his grandmother and enters "into the last dream of Offa the King." In the preceding poems, the poet as child has slipped into identification with Offa while daydreaming, sometimes to return anticlimactically to the schoolyard where "the children boasted their scars of dried snot," at others to retain the royal elevation and impose it on his own world. In one poem, when struck on the head by an apple root, he momentarily becomes the horned Celtic god Cernunnos; otherwise, it is Offa who supplies the ego-ideal. Offa has the attributes a boy might covet, fame, wealth, power, and a GT car, an accessory that bestows status on English youth, hankered after, perhaps, by the young Geoffrey Hill whose father was the police constable of a West country village. In number 10, the boy as king at the royal desk, dispatching royal business, becomes the boy at his own desk doing homework. The poem is headed "Offa's Laws" and opens with a description of the desk. The second part mentions some of the official business transacted at the desk, using a few portentous latinisms:

> It was there that he drew upon grievances from the
> people; attended to signatures and retributions

—activities that a child might imagine as the kingly function. The third part of the poem leads specifically back to the point of view of the child:

> What should a man make of remorse, that it might
> profit his soul? Tell me. Tell everything to
> Mother, darling, and God bless.

The final part contrasts the freedom of daydreaming to work:

> He swayed in sunlight, in mild dreams. He tested the
> little pears. He smeared catmint on his palm for
> his cat Smut to lick. He wept, attempting to mas-
> ter *ancilla* and *servus*.

The poem has moved from official acts of Offa to the private acts of a boy doing homework, from the use of latinisms to the frustration over the mastery of Latin, from the service of the king—the grievances of his people—to the idea of *ancilla* and *servus,* a motif brought up in the epigraph to the poem, which appears in the André Deutsch edition but not in *Somewhere Is Such a Kingdom* and which considers the subject of government and the difference between a man's acting for himself and acting for others.

The poet descends regularly to childhood, to its warmth and security, to the easy availability of forgiveness and innocence. In the twenty-second poem, Hill recalls that warmth and security—amid the contrasting images of war:

> At home the curtains were drawn. The wireless boomed
> its commands. I loved the battle-anthems and the
> gregarious news.

(During World War II, the BBC's nine o'clock news on Sunday evenings was preceded by the national anthems of all the Allies.)

> Then, in the earthy shelter, warmed by a blue-glassed
> storm-lantern, I huddled with stories of dragon-
> tailed airships and warriors who took wing im-
> mortal as phantoms.

Having thus gathered the innocence of childhood, the poet comes grandly back into the present as Offa, whose dominion endures, as we have seen, into the middle of the twentieth century.

A number of the hymns present artifacts: the desk, "brown-oak inlaid with ebony"; the tapestry, "the silver veining, the gold leaf"; the Frankish sword, "the crux a craftsman's triumph"; the coins. Some of the hymns present the act of creation, analogous to the poetic act. In Hill's earlier poems, the poetic act brings its creations from the past, as in "Funeral Music," or from the soil, as in "The lily rears its gouged face / From the provided loam," and burnishes them. In the hymns, however, creations from the earth and the past are joined; the coins in number 13 provide one example.

> Trim the lamp; polish the lens; draw, one by one, rare
> coins to the light. Ringed by its own lustre, the
> masterful head emerges.

The creative act is signaled also by the presence of men working in the earth; in number 12, they dig up a hoard of treasure. Men with dirty boots are present in the second part of 23, following the description of the tapestry in the first part, tapestry and working men relating to creation. Finally, in the last poem, summing up essential relationships, coins and traces of red mud are left behind as Offa vanishes:

> he vanished
>
> he left behind coins, for his lodging, and traces of
> red mud.

The hymns repeatedly return to images of earth—soil, compost, and ditch—and to the creatures of earth—worm, badger, and mole; there is always digging or burrowing among roots. Indeed, the child's kingdom is most often underground, regularly earthy, as in the "earthy shelter" in the quotation above (which portrays an air-raid shelter, presumably). In number 5 we read, "I wormed my way heavenward for ages amid barbaric ivy, scrollwork of fern." The thirteenth shows the child emerging from earth to become the king, a poetic act.

> Far from his underkingdom of crin-
> oid and crayfish, the rune-stone's province, *Rex
> Totius Anglorum Patriae,* coiffured and ageless,
> portrays the self-possession of his possession,
> cushioned on a legend.

The image of Offa in these lines is the one on the coin. In the Mercian hymns, coins are, first, among the famous legacies of King Offa's reign, and they bear an imprint of his head. Second, they are frequently the treasure hoarded underground. Note, for example, the presence underground of the gold solidus (a Roman coin) in number 4, the heading of which is "The Crowning of Offa," a poem in which *invested* is rich in meanings.

> I was invested in mother-earth, the crypt of roots
> and endings. Child's play. I abode there, bided my
> time: where the mole
>
> shouldered the clogged wheel, his gold solidus.

The same motif of underground wealth appears in poem number 6, "The Childhood of Offa," which echoes the rhythms of Dylan Thomas's "Fern Hill" and suggests a complex relationship between active and passive participation in the events of time and the things of the world:

> The princes of Mercia were badger and raven. Thrall
> to their freedom, I dug and hoarded.

Coins are related to another feature of the poetry. In earlier poems the pain of poetic creation is often associated with the attempt to break out of confinement. In "God's Little Mountain," from *Somewhere Is Such a Kingdom,* the speaker says he "was shut / With wads of sound into a sudden quiet." In "The Bidden Guest," from the same volume, the poet speaks of Pentecost:

> I believe in the spurred flame
> Those racing tongues, but cannot come
> Out of my heart's unbroken room.

Often the poet's sense of being pent up is associated with riches: he is shut up guarding a hoard. Alternating with this sense is that of release, and these two create a rhythm that becomes familiar throughout the volumes, in which images of confinement and pressure repeatedly precede those of relief. Hill has spoken of the wonderful sense of consummation and release that lasts for four or five seconds when a poem is completed. But the completed poem is still important to him: he is not finished with it when it is finished; he broods over it still. Hill is unlike Basil Bunting in this regard, who can say of his own completed work that once it's made, he's done with it. Another early poem found in the *Somewhere Is Such a Kingdom,* "Solomon's Mines," contains the characteristic imagery in its characteristic pattern: there is an underground hoard of riches and there is the sense of restraint and confinement. The poem opens with the line, "Anything to have done!" and closes as follows:

> Anything to get up and go
> (Let the hewn gates clash to)
> Without looking round
> Out of that strong land.

The image cluster of restraint and money may conceivably be related to the parts of the repeated word *Pentecost, pent* and *cost,* in spite of its proper etymology—a suggestion that will not be thought overreaching by those who have noted Hill's constant and profound use of puns and the depths of meaning that can be plumbed in individual words.

The pattern of hoarding, of confinement and restraint, followed by release, is even more clear with "In Memory of Jane Fraser," also in *Somewhere Is Such a Kingdom.* In the first three of the four stanzas, the images of immobility and confinement prevail: cold weather, "She kept the siege," the room, "Her body froze." In the last stanza come movement and release:

> In March the ice unloosed the brook
> And water ruffled the sun's hair.
> Dead cones upon the alder shook.

In a volume in which meaning is hidden away like the miser's coin, this poem is relatively clear and the clarity may account for its disfavor in the eyes of the poet.

The coincidence of the pattern of restraint and release with images of treasure, coins, and corpses, and, in turn, the Freudian association of these last with feces, has a significance worth noting. The coincidence appears occasionally in Hill's poems or is hinted at in the overtones of brief passages; in "Requiem for the Plantagenet Kings," for example, "the sea / Across daubed rock evacuates its dead." The act of poetry itself is at times a part of this cluster of images. In "History as Poetry," Pentecost appears, then the corpse, and then dung:

> Poetry as salutation; taste
> Of Pentecost's ashen feast. Blue wounds.
> The tongue's atrocities. Poetry
> Unearths from among the speechless dead
>
> Lazarus mystified, common man
> Of death. The lily rears its gouged face
> From the provided loam. Fortunate
> Auguries; whirrings; tarred golden dung.

The last phrase recalls Freud's reference to Babylonian doctrine that regarded gold as the dung of hell.

Mercian Hymns, with the predominance of the coin images, also reveals these associations, which may serve to link the parts of individual hymns. Coins have already been seen in association with corpses in number 11. Number 12 presents a digging that is both an excavation for treasure and a utilitarian plumbing job. In the first part, "Their spades grafted through the variably-resistant soil. They clove to the hoard." In the second, "The men were paid to caulk water-pipes." These men have a latrine, and in the third part of the poem, describing the condition of the garden and bringing together the two earlier parts, the poet declares, "I have accrued a golden and stinking blaze."

Release from restraint may take the form of a journey in the Mercian hymns. In the seventh poem, "The Kingdom of Offa," Ceolred has let the poet's valued silver model aeroplane fall through the floorboards "into the rat-droppings and coins," after which the speaker lured him

> down to the old quarries, and flayed
> him. Then, leaving Ceolred, he journeyed for hours,
> calm and alone, in his private derelict sandlorry
> named *Albion.*

In poem 17, "Offa's Journey to Rome," after remembering a quarrel with his father and the curious "Disfigurement of a village-king," the poet finds relief in his sports car: "His maroon GT chanted then overtook. He lavished on the high valleys its *haleine*"—a word, according to Hill's note, taken from *La Chanson de Roland*. Visiting Boethius's dungeon (number 18) he purges himself of violence by violent imaginings:

> He shut his eyes, gave rise to a tower
> out of the earth. He willed the instruments of
> violence to break upon meditation. Iron buckles
> gagged; flesh leaked rennet over them; the men
> stooped, disentangled the body.
>
> He wiped his lips and hands. He strolled back to the
> car, with discreet souvenirs for consolation and
> philosophy.

It is interesting that each occasion on which the poet finds release in a car (or lorry) contains an act of sadism or disfigurement.

This is one of the more curious of the image clusters that link some of the Mercian hymns and other poems in Hill's canon. The hymns are also dependent on the relation of the king's activities to those of the child and of modern England to historic Mercia. The childhood of the poet is superimposed on the childhood of his country, and both are radiant as the poem celebrates England: history is lit by shining, finely cut coins, by tapestry with gold leaf, by a sword reflecting winter sun; the poet's childhood is romantic with badger and raven, the Rolls Royce, the GT, and life in the air raid shelter. All through the work, density and fine reticulations of meanings lend a definite structure to poems—unfashionable techniques, bearing Hill's unfashionably grievous message.

Tenebrae, Hill's latest work, retains some of the features of *Mercian Hymns*. There is, for example, the dwelling on buried things—treasure and corpses in the grotesque rendering of Christian salvation in "A Pre-Raphaelite Notebook"—"Gold seraph to gold worm in the pierced slime." There are occasional images and anecdotes reminiscent of the style established with the hymns. In "Vocations" "The twittering pipistrelle, so strange and close, / plucks its curt flight through the moist eventide." Mostly, however, the images do not recover a visual experience; rather, the words are felt as words with histories, objects themselves, not agencies. The volume is a reversion to the style preceding *Mercian Hymns* (a reversion predicted by Harold Bloom); there are the tight forms, the rich elegance, the inaccessibility.

The condition for the poetry of *Tenebrae*, as for the earlier, is the maintenance of a balancing act between declaration and reticence, between the necessity of arriving at formal verse and the imperative of obscurity. Some of the sequences here are religious meditations, and the balancing is performed in the use of metaphor to bring what is ineffable not quite into expression but toward it. The management is particularly that of St. John of the Cross, whose influence along with that of other Spanish poets is evident throughout this volume. Hill's reticence reflects a comment of St. John's on one of his own poems: "It would be ignorance to think that sayings of love understood mystically such as those of the present stanzas, can be fairly explained by words of any kind."

In the title of the opening poem of *Tenebrae*, "The Pentecost Castle," "Pentecost" carries the sense of harvest, and the wheat being harvested is a figure for Christ at His crucifixion. But the overtones provided by punning are in harmony with some of the hidden meanings of the sequence, in which satisfaction of desire paradoxically resides in satisfaction withheld. The epigraph, taken from one of Yeats's letters, initiates the paradox: "It is terrible to desire and not possess, and terrible to possess and not desire." Hill's strategy here is comparable with that of Roy Fisher in *City*, as he carefully avoids the center in a circumvention that suggests where the center might be.

The poems of the Pentecost sequence are brief: twelve short lines in each, divided into three stanzas. A number of the poems suggest two antiphonal voices. The short lines, mostly end-stopped, the rhymes and half rhymes, the repetitions and rhythms play their important parts. Meanings are brought up sharply at the ends of lines, giving them both an appearance of being definitive and a sense of directness, when in fact the poem is deliberately oblique:

> They slew by night
> upon the road
> Medina's pride
> Olmedo's flower.

The poems dwell on the speaker's relationship with Christ, on Christ's wounds and death, and on the wounds inflicted by Christ on the speaker. But these matters are removed from direct presentation: the desire to avoid possession of that which is desired, to elect the former terror of Yeats's alternatives in the epigraph, is a literary motive. Thus, the poem avoids engagement with its subjects by moving into various fictions. The opening poem, the first stanza of which is quoted above, is an example. The second poem is an allegory in the form of a medieval lyric:

> Down in the orchard
> I met my death
> under the briar rose
> I lie slain.

Most remarkable, however, in this tactic of artistic indirection is the removal of the subject matter into erotic terms in the manner practiced by St. John. From his prison cell, St. John heard a snatch of song from a street singer,

> I am dying of love,
> darling, what shall I do?

and was inspired to use erotic idiom in his divine poems. So in Hill,

> This love will see me dead
> he has the place in mind
> where I am free to die
> be true at last true love

and

> Married and not for love
> you of all women
> you of all women
> my soul's darling my love.

St. John calls God *carillo,* darling.

The lowest stage of the speaker's relationship to Christ is arrived at in the seventh poem. Hill is again indebted to St. John, in paticular to "Dark Night," the poem on which St. John wrote his lengthy commentaries, "The Ascent of Mt. Carmel" and "The Dark Night of the Soul"; Christ's darkness, because it is devastating in the privation of all earthly things, is the rich ground for the union of the soul with God:

> Christ the deceiver
> took all I had
> his darkness ever
> my fair reward.

Here is the beginning of an ascent, by lines with increasingly dominant rhymes, culminating in poem 13, in which paradoxes are triumphantly arrayed in lines rhyming or half rhyming in fours, with one notable exception.

> Splendidly-shining darkness
> proud citadel of meekness . . .
>
> and soul for soul discover
> no strangeness to dissever
> and lover keep with lover
> a moment and for ever.

Thus go the beginning and the end of the poem, the rhymes providing an assertion so brazen as to arouse skepticism. The last two poems of the sequence return to the faltering conclusion that consummation of desire is an impossibility, though desire is the condition of this poetry. Yet in its ambiguity, the poem arrives at union: we do not know whether the words are the speaker's or Christ's:

> I shall go down
> to the lovers' well
> and wash this wound
> that will not heal
>
> beloved soul
> what shall you see
> nothing at all
> yet eye to eye
>
> depths of non-being
> perhaps too clear
> my desire dying
> as I desire.

We are attuned by this time to find that the "nothing" that is seen is everything and "non-being" fullness.

ERIC GRIFFITHS

Being in Error

Stephen Dedalus was a young hope-
ful. When John Eglinton suggests that Shakespeare made a mistake in
marrying Ann Hathaway, he replies: "A man of genius makes no mistakes.
His errors are volitional and are the portals of discovery." What this declaration of the rights of supermen seems to mean is that Shakespeare got
married as an experiment in character formation and lived in a permanent
state of technological mastery over his own personality, a "fail-safe" monitor
of his own reactions. Presumably, Stephen would have taken it as a sign
of his own genius that a few minutes earlier, expounding his wilful theory
about *Hamlet,* he misquotes the play. (The Ghost does not say the line
"Hamlet, I am thy father's spirit" which Stephen puts in his mouth.)

I don't know what James Joyce thought of the mistake, or even if
he knew it was one; but it would probably be fair to say that, prodigiously
calculating though he was in his writing, the calculations normally allowed
him a boozy latitude of self-forgiveness. *Ulysses* is, after all, a cheery and
fuddled book in appearance, great as the effort was to keep up that appearance—and Joyce might in justice have passed such latitude on to his
creations.

Geoffrey Hill is harder on himself. In the first essay of *The Lords of
Limit* he speaks of being "possessed by a sense of language itself as a man-
ifestation of empirical guilt", and admits that such possession reduces under
scrutiny to "an anxiety about *faux pas,* the perpetration of 'howlers', grammatical solecisms, misstatements of fact, misquotations, improper attribu-
tions." He frets and sorrows over what comes home to him as the strain
of failure in all human discourse, a failure most sharply instanced in small

From *Encounter* 2, vol. 63 (July/August 1984). Copyright © 1984 by Encounter Ltd.

faults just because they are in themselves not very significant. There is a possible analogy with a theologian who might find that venial sins laid more bare the tottering state of the human will by their diminutive inevitability than greater and more escapable wickednesses. This anxiety, and the answering conduct (Hill reads proofs meticulously, his quotations are from the best texts available, his footnotes minutely careful) are no less a virtue in him because it is not a virtue that could happily be practised generally at his pitch of intensity.

To err is human, to forgive divine, and, though someone who was prompt to forgive himself errors might be playing God over his own life with a comfortable alacrity, it is necessary to forgive oneself as well as other people for wrong-doing, if only to preserve the distinction between the hunger for righteousness and a greedy zeal for always being in the right. Hill fairly concedes that a comic relaxation may be as apt a response to linguistic slips and minor inaccuracies as his own characteristic, apprehensive rigour. The last essay in the book, "Our Word is Our Bond", treats of the culpability of Ezra Pound for his broadcasts over Rome Radio during World War II. Here error is not in what will seem to some an excessive diffidence about tiny details, but in Pound's unfaltering conviction of the poet's claim to an absolute rectitude of judgment, a belief that the poetic vocation confers a right to pronounce on culture. "A man of genius makes no mistakes", but Pound's manner of believing that took him out of James Joyce's company into that of William Joyce.

Hill's study of this case of "irredeemable error in the very substance and texture of [the artist's] craft and pride" searches the issues involved more profoundly than any previous writing on the subject. One reason why this is so is that he does not set apart "craft" and "pride", but comprehends the vice that may be inherent in skill itself; and he arrives at such comprehension by beginning from the technical mishaps to which writing is prey—*il n'y a qu'un faux pas* from sublimity to the ridiculous, or something worse.

Such pressing consciousness of the "concomitant infelicities of clearing one's meanings at an extreme pitch of concentration and in circumstances of complex difficulty" doesn't make the going easy; but then not even his worst enemy would say that Geoffrey Hill was an easy-going writer. *Mercian Hymns* gives us rich grounds to believe that though Hill was a nice child, he probably wasn't nice and easy. "Dreamy, smug-faced, sick on outings", as the fifth Hymn has it. Behind these lines, we can imagine the coercive pleading of parents: "Now, don't be difficult, Geoffrey." With various accents of bafflement or of teased delight, his readers now reiterate that cry; he is known (*The Fontana Biographical Companion to Modern Thought*) as a "notoriously difficult" poet.

The debate about "difficulty" in modern literature—between champions of the daunting like Lionel Trilling in his essay on "The Fate of Pleasure" and the standard-bearers of enlightened philistinism, amenably unafraid of the "obvious", such as Philip Larkin—seems to me usually to get set up in a misleading way, because it confuses two manners of being difficult. A writer may be difficult through the intellectual onerousness of his works, and in this sense Shakespeare is at least as difficult a writer as Ezra Pound; but there is nothing especially "modern" about such difficulty. Or the writer may be difficult in the ways that not only children can be difficult in ordinary life—by being a stickler for correct procedures where a little laxity would speed things up and smooth them over; by putting the worst construction available on something said or done; by always having one more "Why?" when one has run out of "Because."

There is a difficulty of substance that is willed on the writer by the topics with which he deals; and there is a difficulty of manner, which may at times seem wilfully adopted, but may be unelected, demanded by his endeavour to engage the reader with his own sense of the first kind of difficulty. Hume and Kant, for example, deal with many of the same philosophical problems, and are in this sense equally difficult writers; but Hume adopts an ease of manner which is not difficult in the second sense—indeed it is positively, and perhaps deceitfully, socially ingratiating. Or if we compare two poems about British foreign policy—William Empson's "Courage Means Running" and Philip Larkin's "Homage to a Government"—we can see that the topic considered is in both cases difficult, but that Larkin fabricates formally a casual tone which permits exactly those snap judgments which Empson works to circumvent.

There would be some justification for thinking that this second kind of difficulty—a social awkwardness in the conditions under which literature is received—is distinctively "modern." The evidence Geoffrey Hill has painstakingly amassed in *The Lords of Limit* suggests rather that the problem is constantly acute, though protean in the forms it may take; that it arises from a permanent friction between the writer's attempt to speak representatively for the national community and a recognition of his own fractional position within that community, or from even deeper rifts of attitude to the writer's operation in language:

> those for whom writing is like 'bearing a part in the conversation' must regard with incomprehension those for whom it is 'blindness' and 'perplexity' and . . . those for whom 'composition' is a struggle with dark and

disputed matter will inevitably dismiss as mere worldliness the ability to push on pragmatically with the matter in hand.

That is openly even-handed, but Geoffrey Hill's sympathies throughout this book lie with those who neither possess nor long for what Baudelaire called "that flowing style beloved of the *bourgeoisie.*" Hill's poetic work, so stubbornly quarrying in the societal history of word and cadence, inclines him to a social touchiness as regards language, and his is capable of making it look as if the only alternative to his combative sensitivity is tactlessness.

It might be countered that a grasp of the practical variety of acts of communication lets us know that on one occasion nothing but the most strenuous delicacy in handling our words with a maximal sense of their weight of possible tendentiousness will do, and on other occasions we need rather the courage of good humour to give and take words lightly: sometimes, that is, you may be writing the sort of poem Hill writes, and sometimes you may be passing the time of day. But to this I imagine he would reply that my notion of practical grasp merely cloaks an acquiescence in the received usages of society—an acquiescence which needs watching because the clubbable man may turn out to be a quisling. So he writes, for example,

> It may be agreed that in such locutions as, say, 'the language of polite letters' more is implied than 'the methods of combination of words.' Such a 'language' is in fact a 'code' of acceptances, a consensus of taste or prejudice.

Hill's brilliant essays on T. H. Green and Gerard Manley Hopkins provide excellent reasons for suspecting the "off-the-peg" convenience of an unexamined consensus in language, as when he quotes the economist Alfred Marshall's claim that economic studies "call for and develop the faculty of sympathy, and especially that rare sympathy which enables people to put themselves in the place, not only of their comrades, but also of other classes", and takes a bead on that "in the place." While acknowleding that "such phrasing is so much part of innocuous common parlance that to object is a sign only of hermetic irritability", Hill rightly trusts to his vexation and observes the way the fluency of the phrase surreptitiously offers a guarantee of the facility of the process Marshall is describing, a facility we might well have doubts about:

> And there is, in this form of illicit persuasiveness, a hint of the despotic . . . it is less a matter of language living in usage than of usage perching and hatching parasitically upon the surface of language.

That glancing metaphoric vision of usage as a scabies of language typifies the vivid brevity of Hill's critical writing at its best. It offers a rebuke to those who imagine that linguistic permissiveness which recognises no standard of usage, because usage is a law unto itself (I am thinking of Professor Randolph Quirk), is merely an expression of cultural generosity, without noticing that here too permissiveness may afford opportunities for exploitation. Criticism of such sharpness requires a capacity for being nettled by words, and that capacity is a sign of an inability to be (calmly indifferent to the daily laxities of talk. This may be) a hypersensitive morbidity, but then, as Saint Augustine wrote, "hardness does not necessarily imply rectitude, and insensibility is not a guarantee of health."

The same ear which operates in Hill's poetry, with its exceptional range and finesse of dictions antagonistic and reconciled, works in the criticism too, catching turns and wobbles of phrase across a gamut of writing wider than that normally dealt with by "literary" criticism.

A political petition of 1648 helps to illuminate the rhetoric of Jonson's Roman plays, or a declaration of the Nottingham branch of the United Committee of Framework-Knitters combines with Wordsworth's "Ode: Intimations of Immortality . . ." to give a startlingly original and persuasively insightful context for Gerard Manley Hopkins' rhythmic practice.

That last instance again displays Hill's major strength as a critic— a determined prickliness about the social *mores* of language which his intelligence succeeds in turning from bad temper into the sophisticated attunement of an equable temperament in face of its own language. When he writes that "Social locutions which to others might be scarcely more than half-comic irritants impose upon the Nottingham framework-knitters a force as shiftless as that of nature itself," and shows the detailed reciprocal pressure of word and work, he achieves an intimate understanding of the relations of imagination and social actuality. In comparison, all the English Marxist criticism I know which addresses itself to similar questions appears linguistically ham-fisted as well as theoretically hamstrung. He earns of his readers at such moments the admission that Auden makes in the poem from which *The Lords of Limit* takes its title:

> We know you moody, silent, sensitive,
> Quick to be offended, slow to forgive,
> But to your discipline the heart
> Submits when we have fallen apart
> Into the isolated personal life.

The Lords of Limit is the most important first book of criticism by a major English poet since *The Sacred Wood*. It has little of the *brio* of T. S. Eliot's book, but that is not only because Eliot was a jollier soul than Geoffrey Hill. Asking himself why he wrote criticism, Eliot remarked: "The creative artist in England finds himself compelled, or at least tempted, to spend much of his time and energy in criticism that he might reserve for the perfecting of his proper work: simply because there is no one else to do it." His "simply" sounds blithe nowadays; there are plenty of people doing criticism in departments of English up and down the country. The critical air is thick with exegesis, annotation, and the acrimony of scholarly dispute. (Putting it that way sounds only despondent about the industry of academic commentators, which is not my point.)

Hill's criticism effects a substantial, and thoroughly substantiated, reappraisal of the concept of "mastery" as it is used in criticism. The implications of his work are more consequential for literary criticism than that of anyone writing literary criticism in the last half-century (apart from William Empson). But the language of his criticism too often colludes with the "magisterial" just in the instant that it questions the "masterly"; Hill's admirable profundity of apprehension of the ways in which words may be mis-taken is wronged by a professionalised wariness about being taken amiss.

All the show of academic punctilio parades in these pages, with a studied impeccability of manner which I suspect of being reproachful and jokey in the style of Jeeves. What is one to make of the fact that this great poet is so inertly addicted to the double-negative when he writes as a critic (for the pages are littered with "a not unfamiliar modernist theory" and "not unreasonable to suppose" and "not without significance" and "not infrequently")? Or of the recurrent "It is at least open to suggestion", which demurely introduces suggestions of a breathtaking and bracing critical audacity? It may be that the integrity of "scruple" inevitably cooperates in major writing with the canny nervousness of "strategy" ("scruple" and "strategy" come next to each other on pp. 5 and 90), but the style of much of this book concedes so much to merely institutionalised proprieties that it runs the risk of making its vital scruples look merely strategic.

Geoffrey Hill has had to earn his living by being an academic, but he is not an academic critic. Consider the phrase from Bacon which gives him the title of one of the essays in this book: "the true conduct of human judgment." Compare that with Leavis's phrase, adopted from Johnson: "the common pursuit of true judgment." Leavis looks doubly confident in contrast to Hill—his critical pursuit is shared ("common") and it terminates in correctness ("true judgment"). Hill's endeavour experiences more tremor about the communal quest (how perpetually cautious one must be to separate "*true* conduct" from a businesslike acceptance of methods which might be no more than a fund of funded misconduct), and looks more askance at the promised results ("human judgment", which, being human, has its being in error).

Proust misquotes often as a critic because he quotes from memory, and that is all right because he has given us such compelling reasons for being interested in his memory, vagaries included, outside his criticism; Eliot allowed a misquotation of Tourneur to stand from *The Sacred Wood* to the last edition of *Selected Essays* he saw through the press, and beyond. It is a sign of Hill's humility that he doesn't grant himself such license as genius may claim in these matters, but that shouldn't disguise from us the fact that it is with Eliot and Proust that he belongs as a critic, and not with the lesser worthies.

One extraordinary privilege of genius is to create the atmosphere of conversation within a resistant medium, but this Hill's criticism, unlike his poetry, fails to do. Fails, I think, because of a false valuation of correctness and an uncharacteristically one-sided imagination of what conversation is like. All the emphasis in this book falls on speech as an ease and a social fluency, and on the activity of the writer as a "dogged resistance" to the assumptions and presumptuousness of such ease. If we remember Stephen Dedalus in *Ulysses* and his embattled elaboration of a dubious theory about *Hamlet*, it will not seem that all the comfort belongs to those who bear a part in the conversation and all the agonised struggle to the writer. The episode in *Ulysses* in which the characters make play with Shakespeare while Joyce arranges allusions to his plays—so that it seems as true to say that Shakespeare is quoting them as that the characters quote him—may stand as an emblem of Hill's book. Unlike each other as the wilfully erroneous Stephen and the wilfully accurate Hill are, they each engage in the critical game with, as Hill writes of *Cymbeline*, "an edgy watchfulness to the play's virtuosity." The *Ulysses* episode ends:

> Cease to strive. Peace of the druid priests of Cymbeline,
> hierophantic: from wide earth an altar.

> Laud we the gods;
> And let our crooked smokes climb to their nostrils
> From our bless'd altars.

The Lords Of Limit also turns to these lauds with a keener sense of their limitations:

> The poetry is both plangent and jagged. 'Should not the smoke of an acceptable sacrifice rise undeviously to the heavens?' It is a proper question. Cymbeline's command makes an uncontrollable element appear deliberate, converting the accidental and the thwart into a myth of order and direction.

The tribute Hill pays in his writing to "the accidental and the thwart" demands a grateful recognition, even if he has been less able in his criticism than in his poetry to make such tribute the substance of his words. Crooked smoke, perhaps, but there is still life in the old hope that "the crooked shall be made straight, and the rough ways shall be made smooth."

JOHN HOLLANDER

"The Mystery of the Charity of Charles Péguy"

Geoffrey Hill's new sequence, *The Mystery of the Charity of Charles Péguy* (Oxford University Press, New York), published in England last year, has some affinities with his *Tenebrae* sonnets of some years ago. But their Arthurian ambiance (and their powerful parrying of Tennyson, kept just at bay) is superseded in this new poem by the *matere*—as the medievalists call it—of World War I, the poetic province of Brooke and Owen and Rosenberg and other poets of their generation on the one hand, and David Jones's *In Parenthesis* on the other. It exemplifies several senses of the phrase that gives its title to one of Hill's essays, which characterized poetry as "menace and atonement"; its own title alludes to Péguy's *Le Mystère de la charité de Jeanne d'Arc* (she was a central figure in that French writer's three long poems), and it is concerned with the consequences of poetic and spiritual vocation, with the poetic tropes of action and their literalization into violence. Péguy is, for Hill's poem, a version of one of his own *saints-innocents*. The socialist and "self-expatriate but adoring" Catholic (as Hill puts it in a note) had engaged in violent polemic against his sometime Dreyfusard ally, Jean-Léon Jaurès, and whether or not as a consequence of this, the latter was assassinated in a café in 1914, at the brink of the outbreak of the war. That same year, Péguy was killed in a beetfield on the first day of the Battle of the Marne.

Hill's poem starts out with a shot that resounds within the work with greater consequences than the one at Sarajevo:

From *The Yale Review*, vol. 74 (Autumn 1984). Copyright © 1984 by Yale University.

> Crack of a starting-pistol. Jean Jaurès
> dies in a wine-puddle. Who or what stares
> through the café-window crêped in powder-smoke?
> The bill for the new farce reads *Sleepers Awake*.
>
> History commands the stage wielding a toy gun,
> rehearsing another scene. It has raged so before,
> countless times; and will do, countless times more,
> in the guise of supreme clown, dire tragedian.
>
> In Brutus' name martyr and mountebank
> ghost Caesar's ghost, his wounds of air and ink
> painlessly spouting. Jaurès' blood lies stiff
> on menu-card, shirt-front and handkerchief.
>
> Did Péguy kill Jaurès? Did he incite
> the assassin? Must men stand by what they write
> as by their camp-beds or their weaponry
> or shell-shocked comrades while they sag and cry?

One of the masterful things about this sequence is the way in which it can start out with a moral question which most writers would have had to struggle, in the course of a work, to derive: these opening lines cut to the heart of the matter of atonement, for which poetry must make its own pledge of unification. Hill's other, more familiar mastery is apparent everywhere in his firm stanzas, quatrains that move through their own purgatorial changes of rhyme-scheme and frame that superbly tough and resonant diction which this major poet has made his own. Time and again he will strike overtones of the pitch of loaded words, never with the crude ironic purposes of debunking, but in a more autumnal kind of sadness. Thus in a 1914 battlefield scene:

> Inevitable high summer, richly scarred
> with furze and grief; winds drumming the fame
> of the tin legions lost in haystack and stream!
> Here the lost are blest, the scarred most sacred:

he works up glimpses of shattered heroics that go beyond Wilfred Owen's simple "old lie" of *dulce et decorum est,* the "guerdon" which becomes embodied in needless loss ("Chinese" Gordon dying at Khartoum), the phonetic withering of "patience":

> solitary bookish ecstasies, proud tears,
> proud tears, for the forlorn hope, the guerdon
> of Sedan, 'oh les braves gens!', English Gordon
> stepping down sedately into the spears.

> Patience hardens to a pittance, courage
> unflinchingly declines into sour rage,
> the cobweb-banners, the shrill bugle-bands
> and the bronze warriors resting on their wounds.

He does this often throughout the sequence of ten odes, "éloge and elegy" both, as the poem puts it, where "lords of life" sadly diminished from Emerson's move through the inexorable powers of "the lords of limit"—a phrase of Auden's that Hill uses as the title of a splendid book of essays. We hear these reductions in

> of Normandie and Loire. Death does you proud,
> every heroic commonplace, 'Amor',
> 'Fidelitas', polished like old armour,
> stamped forever into the featureless mud.

> push on, push on!—through struggle, exhaustion,
> indignities of all kinds, the impious Christian
> oratory, 'vos morituri', through berserk fear,
> laughing, howling, 'servitude et grandeur'.

The sequence keeps coming back to the contention between the cycles of violent action and verbal fiction:

> No wonder why
> we fall to vioilence out of apathy,
> redeemed by falling and restored to grace
> beyond the dreams of mystic avarice.

> But who are 'we', since history is law,
> clad in our skins of silver, steel and hide,
> or in our rags, with rotten teeth askew,
> heroes or knaves as Clio shall decide?

> 'We' are crucified Pilate, Caiaphas
> in his thin soutane and Judas with the face
> of a man who has drunk wormwood. We come
> back empty-handed from Jerusalem

> counting our blessings, honestly admire
> the wrath of the peacemakers, for example
> Christ driving the money-changers from the temple,
> applaud the Roman steadiness under fire.

> We are the occasional just men who sit
> in gaunt self-judgment on their self-defeat,
> the élite hermits, secret orators
> of an old faith devoted to new wars.

> We are 'embusqués', having no wounds to show
> save from the thorns, ecstatic at such pain.
> Once more the truth advances; and again
> the metaphors of blood begin to flow.

There is a strange touch of Auden in the fourth stanza here, but nobody save Hill could elicit the ironic nuances of "for example . . . temple." This is a passionate and controlled elegy for a major mode of heroic poetry and for the celebration of active ideals (again, I think of Auden, as Hill seldom makes one do, in his setting poetry its task: "Teach the free man how to praise"). Like all modern poetry, this is grounded in its retractions (and lit by the bonfires where the falsefaces of nobility are burned). But these retractions are themselves of imaginative proportions that are as heroic as things get.

Chronology

1932   Geoffrey Hill born in Bromsgrove, Worcestershire, on June 18.
1950   Enters Keble College, Oxford. Graduates with first-class honors in 1953.
1952   Fantasy Press, Oxford, publishes Hill's first volume of poems.
1953   Graduation from Oxford with first-class honors.
1959   *For the Unfallen* published.
1961   Wins the Eric Gregory Award.
1964   *Preghiere.*
1966   *Penguin Modern Poets* 8 issue, with Edwin Brock and Stevie Smith.
1968   *King Log.*
1969   Awarded the Hawthornden Prize.
1971   *Mercian Hymns.*
1972   Heinemann Award. Becomes a Fellow of the Royal Society of Literature.
1975   *Somewhere is Such a Kingdom: Poems, 1952–1971.*
1979   *Tenebrae.*
1983   *The Mystery of the Charity of Charles Péguy.*

Contributors

HAROLD BLOOM, Sterling Professor of the Humanities at Yale University, is the author of *The Anxiety of Influence, Poetry and Repression* and many other volumes of literary criticism. His forthcoming study, *Freud: Transference and Authority*, attempts a full-scale reading of all of Freud's major writings. He is the general editor of *The Chelsea House Library of Literary Criticism*. Among his awards is a MacArthur Foundation Prize Fellowship.

WALLACE D. MARTIN teaches at the University of Toledo. He writes widely on contemporary criticism and on modern poetry.

JON SILKIN is a British poet and critic. His books include *The Peaceable Kingdom* and *Poems New and Selected*.

STEPHEN UTZ is a poet, and also writes film criticism.

SEAMUS HEANEY, who shares with Geoffrey Hill the eminence of being the leading poet in contemporary Great Britain and Ireland, teaches part of the year at Harvard. His books include *Poems: 1965–1975, Field Work* and *Preoccupations*.

CHRISTOPHER RICKS is Professor of English at Cambridge University. He has written studies of Milton, Tennyson and Keats, and edited Tennyson's poetry.

WILLIAM S. MILNE is the author of *The Completest Mode*.

MERLE BROWN teaches at the University of Iowa. He is the editor of the *Iowa Review*, and author of *The Double Lyric* and a study of Wallace Stevens.

CALVIN BEDIENT teaches English at the University of California at Berkeley. He is the author of *Eight Contemporary Poets* and a study of Robert Penn Warren's poetry.

A. K. WEATHERHEAD teaches English at the University of Oregon. He is the author of *The British Dissonance* and *The Edge of the Image*.

JOHN HOLLANDER, poet and critic, teaches Renaissance English literature at Yale University. His books include *Spectral Emanations: New and Selected Poems, Rhyme's Reason* and *The Figure of Echo*.

Bibliography

Agenda 1, vol. 17 (1979). Special issue on Geoffrey Hill.

Alexander, Michael. *"Mercian Hymns."* *Agenda* 3, vol. 13 (1975): 29–30.

Brown, Merle. *Double Lyric: Divisiveness and Communal Creativity in Recent English Poetry.* New York: Columbia University Press, 1980.

Getz, Thomas H. "Geoffrey Hill's *Mercian Hymns* and *Lachrimae*: The Languages of History and Faith." *Modern Poetry Studies* 10 (1980): 2–21.

Glover, John. "The Poet in Plato's Cave: A Theme in the Work of Geoffrey Hill." *Poetry Review*, 3, vol. 69 (March 1980): 60–64.

Hart, Henry. *"The Mystery of the Charity of Charles Péguy*: A Commentary." *Essays in Criticism* 4, vol. 33 (October 1983): 312–38.

Knottenbelt, E. M. "Geoffrey Hill's Silent Songs." *Dutch Quarterly Review* 4, vol. 12 (1982): 246–61.

Launchbury, Michael. "Geoffrey Hill's *Mercian Hymns*." *Delta* 50 (Spring 1972): 44–47.

Milne, William S. "Geoffrey Hill's *Mercian Hymns*." *Ariel* 1, vol. 10 (January 1979): 43–63.

———. " 'Images of Earth and Grace': Geoffrey Hill's *The Mystery of the Charity of Charles Péguy*." *Agenda* 3, vol. 21 (1983): 12–23.

Sisson, C. H. "Geoffrey Hill." *Agenda* 3, vol. 13 (1975): 23–28.

Webb, Igor. "Speaking of the Holocaust: The Poetry of Geoffrey Hill." *The Denver Quarterly* 1, vol. 12 (Spring 1977): 114–24.

Acknowledgments

"Introduction" by Harold Bloom from *Somewhere Is Such a Kingdom* by Geoffrey Hill, copyright © 1976 by Harold Bloom. Reprinted by permission.

"Beyond Modernism" by Wallace D. Martin from *Contemporary Literature* 4, vol. 12 (Autumn 1971), copyright © 1971 by the Regents of the University of Wisconsin. Reprinted by permission.

"The Poetry of Geoffrey Hill" by Jon Silkin from *British Poetry Since 1960*, edited by Michael Schmidt and Grevel Lindop, copyright © 1972 by Jon Silkin. Reprinted by permission.

"The Realism of Geoffrey Hill" by Stephen Utz from *The Southern Review* 2, vol. 12 (Spring 1976), copyright © 1976 by Louisiana State University. Reprinted by permission.

"An English Mason" by Seamus Heaney from *Critical Inquiry* 3, vol. 3 (Spring 1977), copyright © 1977 by The University of Chicago Press. Reprinted by permission.

" 'The Tongue's Atrocities' " by Christopher Ricks from *The Force of Poetry* by Christopher Ricks, copyright © 1984 by Christopher Ricks. Reprinted by permission.

" 'Creative Tact': *King Log*" by William S. Milne from *Critical Quarterly* 4, vol. 20 (Winter 1978), copyright © 1978 by Manchester University Press. Reprinted by permission.

"The Idiom of *Mercian Hymns*" by John Needham from *English* 131, vol. 28 (Summer 1979), copyright © 1979 by The English Association. Reprinted by permission.

" 'Funeral Music' " by Merle Brown from *Double Lyric: Divisiveness and Communal Creativity in Recent English Poetry* by Merle Brown, copyright © 1980 by Carolyn Brown. Reprinted by permission.

Index

A

Advancement of Learning (Bacon), 75
Alamein to Zem Zem (Douglas), 75
Alvarez, A., 17
Amores (Ovid), 114, 115
Anabasis (St. John-Perse), 46
"Annunciations," 14, 69, 117
    theme in, 3–7
    view of poetry in, 4, 5
"Annunciations: I," 55
"Annunciations: II," 56
Arnold, Matthew, 16, 100
"Ascent of Mt. Carmel, The" (St. John
    of the Cross), 127
"Asmodeus, I," realism in, 41–43
"Assisi Fragments, The," 69
Auden, W. H., 133, 139, 140
Augustine, Saint, 133

B

Bacon, Francis, 75, 134
Baudelaire, Charles, 13, 95, 132
Beckett, Samuel, 57, 92, 93, 103
Beowulf: An Introduction (Chambers), 36
Bible, in *Mercian Hymns*, 34, 35
"Bidden Guest, The," 123
Blake, William, 1, 2, 3, 6, 9, 10
Bloom, Harold, 125
Boethius, 38
Briggflatts (Bunting), 115
Brooke, Rupert, 137
Bunting, Basil, 101, 115, 123
Burne-Jones, Edward, 53

C

Campanella, Tommaso, 45, 70
Cantos (Pound), 92
Chambers, R. W., 36
Chanson de Roland, La, 125
"Character of the Happy Warrior, The"
    (Wordsworth), 25
City (Fisher), 126

Coleridge, Samuel Taylor, 2, 87
"Commerce and Society, Of," 114
    holocaust in, 57–59
    theme in, 13, 14
*Concise Encyclopedia of English and
    American Poets and Poetry,* 73, 74
"Conscious Mind's Intelligible
    Structure," 70
Consolatione Philosophiae, De (Boethius),
    38
Contrary Experience, The (Read), 26
"Courage Means Running" (Empson),
    131
Crow (Hughes), 17
Cymbeline (Shakespeare), 135

D

"Dark Night of the Soul" (St. John of
    the Cross), 127
Davie, Donald, 71, 101
Davies, John, 44
"Death of Offa, The," 120
Desnos, Robert, 70
"Distant Fury of Battle, The," 61
"Domaine Public," 69
    holocaust in, 57
Douglas, Keith, 75
"Dover Beach," 99
dramatic lyric, in "Funeral Music," 89–
    100
Dryden, John, 84

E

Eberhart, Richard, 1, 3
Eichmann, Adolf, 24
Eliot, T. S., 13, 15, 21, 43, 63, 84, 92–
    95, 100, 107, 108, 113, 115,
    133–35
    compared to Hill, 92–95, 100
Emerson, Ralph Waldo, 139
Empson, William, 131, 134
"End of a War, The" (Read), 25, 26

F

Fables of Aesop, 75
"Fate of Pleasure, The" (Trilling), 131
"Fern Hill" (Thomas), 122
Fisher, Roy, 126
Flashpoint (Shaw), 69
Fontana Biographical Companion to Modern Thought, 131
For the Unfallen, 1, 10, 12, 14, 102
Fors Clavigora (Ruskin), 47, 52
"Four Poems Regarding the Endurance of Poets," 45, 46
Four Quartets (Eliot), 92, 93, 100, 115
Freud, Sigmund, 2, 5
Frye, Northrop, 13
"Funeral Music," 15, 18, 43, 44, 53, 74
    dramatic lyric in, 89–100
    narrative in, 26–29
    sequence in, 94–100
    themes in, 115–17
    view of poet in, 91–94

G

"Genesis," 1, 3, 6, 11, 12, 15, 18, 24, 26
"Ghost Sonata" (Strindberg), 115
Ginsberg, Allen, 17
"God's Little Mountain," 122
Graham, W. S., 101, 162
Gramsci, Antonio, 47
Grien, T. H., 132

H

Hamburger, Michael, 21, 31
Hamlet (Shakespeare), 129, 135
"Happy Warrior, The" (Read), 25, 26
Heaney, Seamus, 102
Hikmet, Nazim, 103
Hill, Geoffrey
    Blake, influence of, 1
    childhood of, 57
    compared to contemporaries, 101, 102
    critical reception to, 69, 70
    critical reputation of, 1
    history, view of, 102–03
    imagination, view of, 55, 56, 71
    as martyrologist, 1, 6
    see also poetry
History (Lowell), 43

"History as Poetry," 14, 55, 69, 91, 123
Hölderlin, Friedrich, 31, 32
holocaust
    Hill's poetry and, 56–61
Holocaust and the Literary Imagination, The, 57
"Homage to a Government" (Larkin), 131
Homberger, Eric, 77
Homer, 4
Hopkins, Gerard Manley, 68, 102, 132, 133
"Hugh Selwyn Mawberley" (Pound), 12, 29
Hughes, Ted, 4, 10, 17, 49, 101
"Humanist, The," 55
Hume, David, 131

I

Iliad (Homer), 60
imagery
    in Hill's poetry, 22–24
    in *Mercian Hymns*, 121, 122, 124, 125
    in *Somewhere Is Such a Kingdom*, 122–124
    in *Tenebrae*, 125
"Imaginative Life, The," 56, 69
Imagist movement, the, 21, 22, 25, 26
In Parenthesis (Jones), 137

J

James, Henry, 114
Jaurès, Jean-Léon, 137
Johnson, Samuel, 86
Jones, David, 137
Jonson, Ben, 55, 133
Joyce, James, 50, 129, 130, 135
Joyce, William, 130

K

Kant, Immanuel, 131
Keats, John, 3, 7
King Log, 10, 26, 46, 91, 102, 111, 114
    syntax in, 69, 70, 72, 73
    thematic tension in, 74, 75
    tradition challenged in, 72, 73
"Kingdom of Offa, The," 124
Kinsella, Thomas, 10, 101, 111
Kipling, Rudyard, 61

L

"Lachrimae," 88
language
    Hill's view of, 46, 47
    in Hill's poetry, 19–21, 28, 29
    in *Mercian Hymns,* 49–53, 77–86,
       106, 107, 118, 119
    in *Mystery of the Charity of Charles
       Peguy,* 138, 139
Larkin, Philip, 57, 98, 101, 103, 131
Later English Romanesque Sculpture
    (Zarnecki), 50
Lawrence, D. H., 39, 79
literary criticism
    Hill's contribution to, 129–36
    of Hill, 55
"Locust Songs," 56
Lorca, Federico Garcia, 22
Lords of Limit, The
    human failure in, 129, 130
    importance of, 133–36
    writing process in, 131, 132
Lowell, Robert, 17, 42, 102
Lukacs, Georg, 41, 105
Lupercal (Hughes), 102

M

MacNiece, Louis, 71
Mallarmé, Stephen, 71
Manicheanism
    in "Funeral Music," 115, 117
Map of Misreading, A (Bloom), 8
Marshall, Alfred, 132
"Martyrdom of Saint Sebastian, The,"
    56, 116
Mead, Matthew, 113
"Memory of Jane Fraser, In," 3, 18, 75, 123
"Men Are a Mockery of Angels," 69
Mercian Hymns, 1, 18, 24, 33–41, 46,
    56, 87, 102, 130
    Biblical language in, 34, 35
    Christian references in, 33–35
    creative act in, 121, 122
    despair in, 105, 106
    history in, 7–9
    idioms in, 78–86
    imagery in, 121, 122, 124, 125
    ironic voice in, 104, 105
    language of, 34, 35, 49–53, 77–86,
       106, 107, 118, 119

    love in, 5, 6
    metaphor in, 82, 83
    public man in, 36–40
    sequence in, 118, 120
    structure in, 8
    style in, 110, 111
    theme in, 8, 9, 85, 86
"Metamorphoses," 12
"Metamorphoses V," 41, 42
metaphor
    in Hill's poetry, 113
    in *Mercian Hymns,* 82, 83
    as sublimation, 2
Milton, John, 8, 99
modernism, 105
Moncrieff, Scott, 84
"More Sonnets at Christmas, 1942"
    (Tate), 114
Murder in the Cathedral (Eliot), 92, 93
*Mystery of the Charity of Charles Péguy,
    The*
    language in, 138, 139
    poetic vocation in, 137
    sequence in, 139, 140

N

Naked Warriors (Read), 26
narrative
    Hill's use of, 26–29
"News for the Delphic Oracle" (Yeats),
    4
Nietzsche, Friedrich, 5
Nosce Teipsum (Davies), 44

O

"Ode: Intimations of Immortality"
    (Wordsworth), 133
Offa, King, 7, 9, 24, 33–39, 104, 106,
    118–20
"Offa's Coins," 119
"Offa's Journey to Rome," 56, 124
"Offa's Laws," 120
"Offa's Sword," 56
Othello (Shakespeare), 89
"Our Word Is Our Bond," 130
"Ovid in the Third Reich," 27, 36, 46,
    49, 114
    holocaust in, 57
    imagery in, 23, 24
Owen, Wilfred, 137, 138

P

Péguy, Charles, 137
Penguin Book of Contemporary Verse, The, 14, 69
Penguin Book of Latin Verse, The, 33, 34
Penguin Modern Poets, 8, 69
"Pentecost Castle, The," 125
philosophy
    in Hill's poetry, 44
"Picture of a Nativity," 44, 45
Plath, Sylvia, 17
Plato, 116
poetry
    "Annunciations," views in, 4, 5
    Eliot's view of, 92, 93
    form, use of, 17–19, 30, 31
    guilt in, 102, 103
    Hill's view of, 14, 15
    holocaust in, 56–61
    human pain in, 1
    imagery, use of, 22–24
    imagination/repression in, 2
    Imagist movement, 21, 22, 25, 26
    language, use of, 19–21, 28, 29, 49–53, 77–86
    metaphor in, 113
    narrative, use of, 26–29
    philosophy in, 44
    punctuation in, 61–67
    puns in, 123
    realism in, 41–47
    sequence in, 113–15
    sublimation in, 2
    symbolist movement, 71
    syntax in, 69, 70, 72, 73
    view of poet in, 91–94
Pope, Alexander, 77, 78, 84
"Postures," 33
Pound, Ezra, 21, 29, 43, 92, 130, 131
"Prayer to the Sun, A," 69
Preghiere, 69
"Pre-Raphaelite Notebook, A," 125
"Processionals in the Exemplary Cave," 91, 92
Proust, Marcel, 135
pun
    Hill's use of, 123

Q

Quirk, Randolph, 133

R

Read, Herbert, 25, 26
realism
    in Hill's poetry, 41–47
Reason and Energy (Holderlin), 31, 32
"Recessional" (Kipling), 61
"Redeeming the Time," 46, 47
"Requiem for the Plantagenet Kings," 53, 123
Ritsos, Yannis, 103
Ruskin, John, 39, 47, 52

S

Sacred Wood, The (Eliot), 133, 135
St. John of the Cross, 125–28
Selected Essays (Eliot), 135
"September Song," 2, 18
    holocaust in, 57
    punctuation in, 64–67
sequence
    in "Funeral Music," 94–100
    Hill's use of, 113–15
    in *Mercian Hymns,* 118, 120
    in *Mystery of the Charity of Charles Péguy,* 139, 140
Serpieri, Alessandro, 100
Shakespeare, William, 53, 89, 131, 135
Shaw, Robert, 69
Shelley, Percy Bysshe, 3, 10, 13
Silkin, Jon, 10, 64–66, 69–71, 83, 87–89, 91
Sisson, C. H., 9, 36, 83, 87–89, 101, 106
Smith, Stevie, 101
"Solomon's Mines," 123
Somewhere Is Such a Kingdom, 41, 114, 117, 118, 120
"Song from Armenia, A," 32, 45
"Songbook of Sebastian Arrurruz, The," 15, 29–33
Spender, Stephen, 71
Stand, 69
Steiner, George, 59
Stevens, Wallace, 8, 71
Sweet's Anglo-Saxon Reader, 33, 34
Swift, Jonathan, 72
Symbolist movement, 71
syntax
    in *King Log,* 69, 70, 72, 73

T

Tate, Allen, 1, 42, 73, 74, 113
Tenebrae, 88, 102, 137
    compared to *Mercian Hymns*, 107
    imagery in, 125
    sequence in, 107–10
    style in, 125
Tennyson, Alfred, Lord, 61, 93, 115,
    137
theme
    in early poems, 3–7
    in "Funeral Music," 115–17
    in Hill's poetry, 11–16
    in *Mercian Hymns*, 8, 9, 85, 86
Thomas, R. S. 101
"Three Baroque Meditations," 41, 42,
    69, 71
Tolstoy, Leo, 89
Tomlinson, Charles, 10, 101
transumption, 8
Trilling, Lionel, 131
"Troublesome Reign, The," 41, 42
T. S. Eliot: le strutture profond (Serpieri),
    100
"Turtle Dove, The," 41, 42
"Two Formal Elegies," 58–66

U

Ulysses (Joyce), 50, 129, 135
Ungaretti, Giuseppe, 21

V

Virgil, 44
"Vocations," 125
Voltaire, 60
"Voyage à Cythère, Un," (Baudelaire),
    13

W

War of the Roses, 116
Waste Land, The (Eliot), 63
Wittgenstein, Ludwig, 47
Women in Love (Lawrence), 89
Wordsworth, William, 3, 8, 9, 10, 25,
    133

Y

Yeats, William Butler, 4, 7, 10, 13, 55,
    70, 126

Z

Zarnecki, G., 51